LLM Agents

A Hands-on Guide to Building Intelligent, Autonomous Systems

©

Written By

Charles Sprinter

Copyright Page

Title: *LLM Agents: A Hands-On Guide to Building Intelligent, Autonomous Systems*
Author: Charles Sprinter
Year of Publication: 2025

Acknowledgments:
The author would like to thank [Name of individuals, institutions, or organizations] for their contributions to the research, writing, and development of this book.

Table of Contents

Preface

1. Author's Note

Welcome to **"LLM Agents: A Hands-on Guide to Building Intelligent, Autonomous Systems."** As the author of this book, I am thrilled to share my knowledge and experience in the rapidly evolving field of artificial intelligence, specifically focusing on Large Language Model (LLM) Agents. My journey in AI began over a decade ago, driven by a passion for understanding how machines can mimic and enhance human intelligence. Throughout my career, I have had the privilege of working on various AI projects, collaborating with brilliant minds, and witnessing firsthand the transformative power of AI technologies.

The motivation behind this book stems from the increasing relevance and potential of LLM Agents in today's digital landscape. With advancements in natural language processing and machine learning, LLM Agents have become pivotal in automating complex tasks, enhancing user experiences, and driving innovation across industries. This book is designed to bridge the gap between theoretical concepts and practical implementation, providing you with the tools and insights needed to build intelligent, autonomous systems that can think, learn, and act independently.

My goal is to equip you with a comprehensive understanding of LLM Agents, from their foundational principles to advanced techniques and real-world applications. Whether you are a developer, researcher, AI enthusiast, or business professional, this book aims to serve as a valuable resource in your AI endeavors.

2. Acknowledgments

Creating this book has been a rewarding and collaborative journey, and I am deeply grateful to everyone who has contributed to its development:

- **My Mentors and Colleagues:** Your guidance, expertise, and unwavering support have been instrumental in shaping my understanding of AI and LLM Agents. Your willingness to share knowledge and insights has enriched this book immensely.
- **The AI Community:** The vibrant and dynamic AI community, including researchers, developers, and practitioners, has provided a

wealth of knowledge and inspiration. Your continuous advancements and open sharing of information have made this book possible.

- **Beta Readers and Reviewers:** Special thanks to the individuals who took the time to review early drafts of this book. Your constructive feedback and suggestions have been invaluable in refining the content and ensuring its quality.
- **Friends and Family:** Your patience, encouragement, and belief in my work have been my anchor throughout this process. Thank you for understanding the long hours and dedication required to bring this book to fruition.
- **Technology Providers:** Gratitude to the platforms, tools, and services that have facilitated the research and development of LLM Agents. Your contributions have enabled practical implementations and real-world applications discussed in this book.

3. How to Use This Book

Intended Audience

This book is crafted for a diverse audience eager to delve into the world of LLM Agents. Whether you are:

- **Developers and Engineers:** Looking to implement LLM Agents in your projects and seeking practical guidance on building intelligent systems.
- **Researchers and Academics:** Interested in the latest advancements, methodologies, and theoretical foundations of LLM Agents.
- **AI Enthusiasts and Students:** Eager to gain comprehensive knowledge and hands-on experience in developing autonomous AI systems.
- **Business Professionals:** Exploring AI applications to enhance operations, improve customer experiences, and drive innovation within your organization.

Each chapter is structured to cater to varying levels of expertise, ensuring that both beginners and seasoned professionals find value in the content.

Book Structure and Features

"LLM Agents: A Hands-on Guide to Building Intelligent, Autonomous Systems" is organized into seven comprehensive parts, each focusing on different aspects of LLM Agents:

- **Part I: Foundations of LLM Agents**
  Establishes the essential concepts, historical evolution, and theoretical underpinnings of LLM Agents.
- **Part II: Designing and Building LLM Agents**
  Guides you through the planning, design, technical integration, and development processes involved in creating LLM Agents.
- **Part III: Advanced Techniques and Optimizations**
  Explores sophisticated methods to enhance the intelligence, autonomy, and performance of LLM Agents.
- **Part IV: Practical Applications and Case Studies**
  Demonstrates real-world applications across various industries, supplemented by detailed case studies.
- **Part V: Ethical, Legal, and Societal Considerations**
  Addresses the ethical implications, legal frameworks, and societal impacts of deploying LLM Agents.
- **Part VI: Future Trends and Innovations**
  Looks ahead to emerging technologies and future developments that will shape the evolution of LLM Agents.
- **Part VII: Additional Essential Topics**
  Covers crucial topics such as user-centric design, troubleshooting, collaborative development, ethical practices, and monetization strategies.

Key Features Include:

- **Hands-On Projects and Exercises:**
  Each chapter includes practical projects and coding exercises that reinforce the concepts discussed, allowing you to apply your knowledge in real-world scenarios.
- **Comprehensive Code Examples:**
  Detailed code snippets and templates are provided to demonstrate the implementation of various functionalities within LLM Agents. All examples are thoroughly explained to ensure clarity and understanding.
- **Visual Aids:**
  Diagrams, flowcharts, and infographics are used extensively to illustrate complex architectures, data flows, and processes, enhancing comprehension and retention.
- **Case Studies:**
  Real-world success stories and case studies showcase the practical applications and benefits of LLM Agents across different sectors, providing inspiration and actionable insights.

- **Supplementary Materials:**
  The appendices, glossary, and references sections offer additional resources, definitions, and readings to support your learning journey.

Companion Resources (Website, Code Repositories, etc.)

To complement the content of this book, a suite of companion resources is available to enhance your learning experience:

- **Companion Website:**
  Accessible at www.llmagentsbook.com, the website serves as a central hub for all supplementary materials. Here, you will find:
  - **Code Repositories:**
    All code examples, templates, and project files discussed in the book are hosted on GitHub. Access them at github.com/llmagentsbook for easy download and collaboration.
  - **Video Tutorials:**
    Step-by-step video guides accompany complex projects and coding exercises, providing visual and auditory explanations to complement the written content.
  - **Interactive Quizzes and Assessments:**
    Test your understanding and reinforce your learning through interactive quizzes available online, designed to evaluate your comprehension of key topics.
  - **Discussion Forums:**
    Engage with fellow readers, ask questions, share insights, and collaborate on projects in our dedicated forums. Participate in discussions and gain diverse perspectives from the AI community.
  - **Regular Updates and Errata:**
    Stay informed about the latest updates, corrections, and enhancements to the book's content. The website is regularly updated to reflect new developments and incorporate feedback from readers.
- **Downloadable Resources:**
  Access a range of downloadable materials, including PDF summaries, cheat sheets, and configuration guides, to support your hands-on projects and study sessions.
- **Newsletter Subscription:**
  Subscribe to our newsletter to receive the latest news, tips, and

exclusive content directly to your inbox. Stay connected and informed about upcoming webinars, events, and new resources.

By leveraging these companion resources, you can maximize your learning potential, engage with a community of like-minded individuals, and stay abreast of the latest advancements in LLM Agents and AI technologies.

Happy reading and building!

Chapter 1: Introduction to LLM Agents

1. What are LLM Agents?

Definition and Key Concepts

LLM Agents are intelligent systems powered by Large Language Models (LLMs), designed to perform tasks autonomously by understanding, processing, and generating human-like language. These agents are capable of interacting with users and other systems, making decisions, and learning from their environment.

At their core, LLM Agents are composed of two main components:

1. **Language Understanding:** The ability to comprehend and interpret input, typically in the form of natural language. This includes recognizing context, meaning, sentiment, and intent in the language.
2. **Action and Response Generation:** After understanding the input, the agent generates appropriate responses or actions. This might include generating text, taking a specific action, or interacting with external systems to achieve a goal.

Key characteristics of **LLM Agents** include:

- **Natural Language Understanding (NLU):** The agent's ability to process and comprehend human language.
- **Natural Language Generation (NLG):** The agent's ability to produce human-like responses.
- **Autonomy:** The capacity to perform tasks without constant human oversight, making decisions based on input, learned patterns, and set goals.
- **Adaptability:** LLM Agents can learn from interactions and adapt to new contexts, improving over time.

LLM Agents have a wide range of applications, from chatbots and virtual assistants to more complex roles in healthcare, finance, and customer support.

Distinction Between LLMs and Traditional AI Agents

To understand the power and versatility of LLM Agents, it's important to compare them with traditional AI agents.

1. **Traditional AI Agents:**
   - **Rule-Based Systems:** Early AI agents often operated based on a set of predefined rules. For example, a chatbot might have been designed to recognize certain keywords and respond with pre-written phrases. These agents typically had a narrow scope and lacked the ability to learn or adapt from user input.
   - **Limited Flexibility:** Traditional AI systems were often inflexible and could handle only very specific tasks.
2. **LLM Agents:**
   - **Learning and Adaptability:** Unlike traditional AI agents, LLMs can learn from vast amounts of text data. They use deep learning techniques to recognize patterns, understand complex contexts, and generate human-like responses.
   - **Context-Aware and Dynamic:** LLM Agents are not limited to rule-based responses. They understand context, are capable of handling ambiguous inputs, and can generate diverse and creative outputs.
   - **Broader Scope:** LLM Agents can handle a wider variety of tasks, including complex language generation, translation, summarization, and even performing reasoning tasks.

In short, **LLM Agents** extend the capabilities of traditional AI agents by enabling dynamic, flexible, and context-aware interactions.

2. Historical Evolution

Early AI Agents

The concept of intelligent agents has been around for decades. Early AI systems were relatively simple and rule-based. These systems used manually programmed rules to perform tasks such as:

- **Expert Systems:** These were designed to simulate the decision-making ability of a human expert. They typically relied on large databases of factual information and an inference engine to apply rules to that data.

- **Chatbots and Conversational Agents:** Early chatbots, like ELIZA (developed in the 1960s), were simple pattern-matching systems designed to mimic human conversation. While innovative for their time, these agents were limited in their ability to understand and generate complex language.

Despite their novelty, early AI agents struggled with understanding the complexities of human language. They required large amounts of manually curated data and lacked the ability to adapt to new or unforeseen situations.

Emergence of Large Language Models

In the 2010s, deep learning techniques, particularly **Transformers** and **Attention Mechanisms**, revolutionized the field of natural language processing (NLP). These breakthroughs led to the development of **Large Language Models (LLMs)** like **GPT-3**, **BERT**, and **T5**.

1. **Transformers and Attention Mechanisms:** The introduction of the Transformer architecture in 2017 marked a turning point in NLP. Unlike previous models that relied on sequential processing, Transformers could process entire sequences of words simultaneously. This allowed for better handling of long-range dependencies and more accurate language modeling.
2. **Pretrained Models:** LLMs like **GPT-3** and **BERT** are pretrained on massive corpora of text data, enabling them to learn grammar, facts, reasoning patterns, and some level of common sense. This pretraining enables them to be fine-tuned for specific tasks with much less labeled data.

With these advancements, LLMs became capable of tasks previously considered out of reach for AI, including:

- Complex text generation
- Question answering
- Translation
- Summarization
- Conversational AI

Integration of LLMs into Agent Architectures

The integration of LLMs into agent architectures has created a new class of **LLM Agents** that are dynamic, adaptable, and capable of learning from interactions. These agents utilize the power of LLMs to perform a variety of tasks autonomously, such as:

- **Personal Assistants:** Virtual assistants that understand and respond to user queries across multiple domains.
- **Customer Support Agents:** AI agents that can answer customer inquiries, provide troubleshooting steps, and even complete transactions.
- **Autonomous Systems:** LLM-powered agents embedded in robotics, healthcare, or financial applications to make decisions, interpret data, and generate human-like responses in real-time.

The shift from static, rule-based systems to LLM-driven agents has dramatically improved the accuracy, versatility, and functionality of AI systems.

3. Importance and Relevance in 2025

Current Trends in AI and LLM Development

As of 2025, LLM Agents are at the forefront of AI development, with several key trends shaping their growth and relevance:

1. **Improved Fine-Tuning Capabilities:** The ability to fine-tune LLMs for specific industries, tasks, and domains is becoming increasingly efficient. Customization of LLMs allows agents to specialize in fields like healthcare, finance, legal services, and entertainment.
2. **Multimodal Models:** Modern LLMs are evolving to handle not just text but also multimodal inputs (e.g., images, audio). This expansion enables more interactive and immersive experiences.
3. **Explainable AI (XAI):** As LLM Agents become more involved in decision-making processes, there is growing demand for transparency and explainability. Researchers are working on techniques to make LLM decisions more interpretable to humans.
4. **Collaboration with Other AI Systems:** LLM Agents are being integrated into multi-agent systems, where they collaborate with other types of AI (e.g., computer vision systems, reinforcement learning agents) to accomplish complex tasks.
5. **Ethical AI Development:** There is increasing focus on ethical considerations when developing LLM Agents, including bias mitigation, fairness, privacy, and accountability. The AI community

is working towards ensuring that LLM Agents are deployed in responsible and sustainable ways.

Market Demand and Industry Applications

LLM Agents have already made significant strides in various industries, and their relevance is expected to continue growing in 2025:

- **Healthcare:** LLM Agents are being used to assist in diagnosing conditions, suggesting treatments, and interacting with patients through virtual assistants.
- **Finance:** AI-driven financial agents are helping with tasks like fraud detection, trading, and customer support in banking.
- **E-commerce and Retail:** Personalized shopping assistants, virtual stylists, and customer service agents powered by LLMs are enhancing the online shopping experience.
- **Education:** Virtual tutors powered by LLM Agents are revolutionizing online learning platforms by providing personalized instruction, grading assignments, and offering study help.
- **Legal Services:** LLMs are aiding in legal research, document analysis, and even contract creation, significantly reducing the time and cost associated with legal work.

The market for LLM Agents is rapidly expanding as organizations seek to automate complex tasks, improve efficiency, and enhance user experience.

4. Overview of the Book

What to Expect in Each Part

This book is divided into seven parts, each designed to take you on a comprehensive journey from understanding the foundations of LLM Agents to implementing and optimizing them in real-world applications.

- **Part I: Foundations of LLM Agents**
  Introduces the concept of LLM Agents, explains their historical development, and discusses their relevance in 2025. It lays the groundwork for understanding the technology and its applications.
- **Part II: Designing and Building LLM Agents**
  Focuses on the practical aspects of designing, building, and deploying LLM Agents. It covers system architecture, development tools, and technical integration.

- **Part III: Advanced Techniques and Optimizations**
  Explores advanced methods for enhancing the intelligence, autonomy, and performance of LLM Agents.
- **Part IV: Practical Applications and Case Studies**
  Provides real-world examples and case studies across various industries, demonstrating how LLM Agents are applied to solve complex challenges.
- **Part V: Ethical, Legal, and Societal Considerations**
  Discusses the ethical, legal, and societal issues surrounding LLM Agents, with a focus on privacy, bias, and accountability.
- **Part VI: Future Trends and Innovations**
  Examines emerging technologies and future developments in AI and LLMs, including multimodal models, quantum computing, and decentralized AI.
- **Part VII: Additional Essential Topics**
  Covers essential topics such as troubleshooting, user-centric design, and monetization strategies.

How to Navigate the Content

Each chapter is designed to build upon the last, so it is recommended to follow the book in sequence for the best learning experience. However, if you are an advanced reader, feel free to skip ahead to the sections that interest you most.

- **Beginner Readers:** Start with the foundational chapters in Part I, and gradually work your way through the technical and application-focused content.
- **Intermediate Readers:** Focus on Parts II and III, which provide hands-on techniques for developing and optimizing LLM Agents.
- **Advanced Readers:** Dive into the cutting-edge content in Part VI, where you'll find discussions on the latest AI trends and the future of LLM Agents.

This book is meant to be a practical guide, and each chapter includes code examples, hands-on exercises, and real-world applications to help you build and refine your own LLM Agents.

Chapter 2: Understanding Large Language Models (LLMs)

1. Fundamentals of LLMs

Large Language Models (LLMs) have emerged as one of the most important advancements in the field of artificial intelligence. They are capable of understanding, generating, and manipulating human language, making them a powerful tool for a wide variety of applications, from conversational agents to creative writing assistants and beyond. To understand LLMs, it's essential to delve into their underlying architecture and components.

Architecture Overview (Transformers, Attention Mechanisms)

The foundation of most modern LLMs, such as GPT-3, BERT, and T5, is the **Transformer architecture**, which was introduced in a seminal paper titled *Attention Is All You Need* by Vaswani et al. in 2017. This architecture revolutionized natural language processing by addressing several limitations of previous models.

The Transformer Model

The Transformer model is based on a **self-attention mechanism** that allows it to process entire sequences of data (e.g., sentences or paragraphs) in parallel, rather than sequentially. This parallel processing significantly speeds up training times compared to older models like Recurrent Neural Networks (RNNs) or Long Short-Term Memory (LSTM) networks, which processed data sequentially.

Key components of the Transformer architecture include:

1. **Encoder-Decoder Structure**:
   - In the original Transformer model, the encoder processes the input data (e.g., a sentence in English), while the decoder generates the output data (e.g., a translation in French).
   - LLMs like GPT-3, however, typically use only the **decoder** part of the Transformer, as they are designed primarily for generating text rather than translation.
2. **Self-Attention Mechanism**:

- The self-attention mechanism allows the model to weigh the importance of each word in a sentence relative to the others. For example, in the sentence *"The cat sat on the mat,"* the word "sat" might be most important in understanding the meaning, and the self-attention mechanism will adjust its focus accordingly.
- This mechanism helps the model capture long-range dependencies in text (e.g., relationships between words that are far apart in a sentence).

3. **Multi-Head Attention**:
   - Multi-head attention is an extension of the self-attention mechanism. It involves using multiple attention heads to look at different parts of the sentence in parallel, allowing the model to capture different kinds of relationships between words.

Attention Mechanism

The attention mechanism computes a weighted sum of input values, where the weights (or attention scores) are learned through training. The attention score determines how much focus each word should have when processing the current word.

For instance, in a sentence like *"The cat sat on the mat,"* the model might focus more on "cat" and "sat" when predicting the next word. This ability to focus attention on relevant parts of the input is what gives Transformer models their power.

Key Components and Layers

LLMs like GPT-3 and BERT consist of several layers of attention and transformation mechanisms. Each layer contains the following components:

1. **Input Embeddings**:
   - Words are converted into vectors of real numbers in a high-dimensional space. These vectors capture semantic information about the words (i.e., words with similar meanings will have similar vector representations).
2. **Positional Encodings**:
   - Since the Transformer model processes input data in parallel, it doesn't have a built-in notion of word order. Positional encodings are added to the input embeddings to provide the

model with information about the order of words in the sentence.

3. **Transformer Blocks**:
   o Each transformer block consists of two main parts:
      ▪ **Multi-Head Self-Attention Layer**: This part focuses on computing the attention scores between all words in the sentence.
      ▪ **Feedforward Neural Network**: After the attention step, the output is passed through a feedforward neural network to further process the information.

4. **Output Layer**:
   o For text generation tasks, the output layer generates the next word (or token) based on the previous words in the sequence.

2. Training LLMs

Training LLMs requires vast amounts of data, computational power, and careful optimization. Here's an overview of the training process:

Data Collection and Curation

The first step in training an LLM is collecting a massive dataset. LLMs are typically trained on diverse corpora that include a wide range of text from the internet, books, scientific articles, and other sources. The dataset must be large and diverse enough to help the model understand the intricacies of human language, including grammar, vocabulary, idiomatic expressions, and factual knowledge.

- **Common Data Sources**: Wikipedia, Common Crawl (a web scrape of billions of web pages), books, research papers, and social media posts.
- **Data Cleaning**: Before training, the data is cleaned to remove irrelevant or harmful content, such as spam or biased information. This step is crucial to ensure the quality and integrity of the training data.

Preprocessing Techniques

Once the data is collected, it undergoes preprocessing to prepare it for training. This process involves:

- **Tokenization**: Splitting the text into smaller units (tokens) like words or subwords. Tokenization is necessary because neural networks work with numerical data, and text data needs to be converted into a numerical format.

  For example, the sentence *"The cat sat"* might be tokenized as:

  - ["The", "cat", "sat"]

  Tokenization allows the model to efficiently handle variable-length text and also aids in handling unknown words by breaking them down into smaller, known parts.

- **Padding**: To ensure that all input sequences are of the same length, shorter sentences are padded with special tokens. This helps batch processing, where multiple sequences are fed into the model at the same time.
- **Normalization**: Text may also be normalized to lower case, remove punctuation, or handle special characters.

Training Algorithms and Optimization

Training LLMs is a highly computationally expensive process that involves optimizing millions or even billions of parameters. Here's how the process works:

1. **Loss Function**:
   - LLMs are typically trained using a **language modeling** objective. This involves predicting the next word in a sequence given the previous words. The loss function measures the difference between the predicted word and the actual word, guiding the model's learning process.
2. **Optimization Algorithms**:
   - **Stochastic Gradient Descent (SGD)** and its variants (e.g., Adam, AdamW) are used to update the model's parameters based on the loss function. These optimization algorithms iteratively adjust the parameters to minimize the loss function, making the model better at predicting the next word in a sequence.
3. **Regularization**:
   - Regularization techniques like **dropout** are employed to prevent the model from overfitting to the training data.

Overfitting occurs when the model becomes too specialized to the training data and performs poorly on unseen data.

4. **Batch Training**:
    o Large-scale models like GPT-3 are trained using **mini-batch** gradient descent, where the model processes a subset of data at a time. This helps with memory efficiency and allows the model to learn from a variety of examples in parallel.

5. **Distributed Training**:
    o Due to the sheer size of LLMs, training is typically done across many GPUs or TPUs in parallel. This approach significantly speeds up the training process and allows the model to scale effectively.

3. Capabilities of LLMs

LLMs are powerful tools due to their ability to process, understand, and generate human language in a variety of ways. Here are the core capabilities of LLMs:

Natural Language Understanding and Generation

- **Text Generation**: One of the most well-known capabilities of LLMs is generating coherent and contextually appropriate text. LLMs can generate entire paragraphs or even pages of text, making them ideal for content creation, creative writing, and conversational agents.

Example (Code for Text Generation using GPT-2):

```
from transformers import GPT2LMHeadModel, GPT2Tokenizer

model = GPT2LMHeadModel.from_pretrained('gpt2')
tokenizer = GPT2Tokenizer.from_pretrained('gpt2')

input_text = "Artificial intelligence is transforming
the world by"
inputs = tokenizer(input_text, return_tensors="pt")

outputs = model.generate(inputs["input_ids"],
max_length=50, num_return_sequences=1)

print(tokenizer.decode(outputs[0],
skip_special_tokens=True))
```

In this example, the model generates a continuation of the given input text, illustrating the text generation capability.

- **Language Understanding**: LLMs excel at understanding the meaning of text, allowing them to perform tasks such as **question answering**, **summarization**, and **information retrieval**. They can comprehend and process complex information, drawing from their training data.

Multimodal Capabilities (Text, Image, Audio Integration)

While most LLMs are focused on text, there is a growing trend to integrate multiple types of data. Some models now have multimodal capabilities, which allow them to handle and generate not just text but also images, audio, and even video.

- **Image and Text Integration**: Some LLMs, like **CLIP** (Contrastive Language-Image Pretraining), can understand both images and text and generate descriptions or captions based on the visual content.
- **Audio and Speech Processing**: Models like **Whisper** can transcribe spoken language into text, bridging the gap between text-based and audio-based communication.
- **Multimodal Applications**: In applications such as virtual assistants, multimodal agents can generate both textual responses and actions (e.g., generating an image or playing an audio clip).

4. Limitations and Challenges

While LLMs have revolutionized many aspects of AI, they still face several challenges that need to be addressed.

Computational Requirements

Training LLMs is computationally expensive and resource-intensive. Models like GPT-3 have billions of parameters, and training them requires vast amounts of computational power, often distributed across multiple GPUs or TPUs.

- **Energy Consumption**: The environmental impact of training LLMs is a growing concern, as large-scale training processes consume significant amounts of energy.

Bias and Ethical Concerns

LLMs are trained on vast amounts of internet data, and as a result, they often inherit biases present in the data. These biases can manifest in harmful ways, such as:

- **Gender, Racial, and Cultural Biases**: LLMs may produce biased or discriminatory outputs that reflect societal stereotypes.
- **Misinformation**: Since LLMs are trained on a wide variety of sources, they may generate content that is inaccurate or misleading.

Mitigation Strategies

To address these challenges, several mitigation strategies are being developed:

1. **Bias Detection and Removal**: Techniques like adversarial training and fine-tuning on curated, balanced datasets can help reduce biases in LLMs.
2. **Model Transparency and Accountability**: Explainable AI (XAI) techniques are being explored to make LLMs' decision-making processes more transparent.
3. **Ethical Guidelines**: Developers are increasingly incorporating ethical frameworks to guide the design and deployment of AI systems, ensuring that LLMs are used responsibly.

This chapter provides a comprehensive overview of Large Language Models (LLMs), covering their architecture, capabilities, and limitations. As you progress through the book, you'll gain a deeper understanding of how to design, develop, and optimize LLM Agents, building on the foundational knowledge of LLMs covered here.

Chapter 3: Theoretical Foundations of AI Agents

Artificial intelligence (AI) agents are systems that can perform tasks autonomously or semi-autonomously by perceiving their environment, reasoning about it, and acting on it to achieve their goals. This chapter will explore the foundational concepts of AI agents, including their characteristics, types, architectures, and levels of autonomy. Understanding these theoretical foundations is essential for anyone looking to design, develop, or deploy intelligent agents in real-world applications, especially in domains like robotics, IoT, and large-scale data analysis.

1. Defining AI Agents

Characteristics and Functionalities

AI agents are defined by their ability to perceive, reason, and act within an environment. There are several defining characteristics and functionalities that make up an AI agent:

- **Perception:** The agent can gather information from its environment using sensors. For instance, a robot might use cameras and microphones to perceive its surroundings, while a software agent might gather data from a web service or database.
- **Reasoning:** The agent can process the information it perceives and use it to make decisions. This often involves logical reasoning, pattern recognition, or machine learning techniques to interpret and analyze the data.
- **Action:** Based on its reasoning, the agent can then take actions to achieve its goals. These actions might include moving, interacting with other agents, or performing specific tasks, such as responding to a query or initiating a process.
- **Autonomy:** AI agents can operate without human intervention. The level of autonomy may vary, with some agents requiring more guidance and others functioning independently in complex environments.
- **Goal-Oriented Behavior:** AI agents are typically designed with specific objectives in mind, such as navigating a physical space, solving a problem, or completing a task. The agent must be able to set and pursue these goals effectively.

- **Adaptability:** Some AI agents can learn from their environment and improve their performance over time. This learning might involve supervised, unsupervised, or reinforcement learning techniques.

Types of Agents

AI agents can be categorized based on how they perceive, reason, and act. The three primary types of agents are:

1. **Reactive Agents:**
   - **Characteristics:** Reactive agents respond to stimuli in their environment without maintaining an internal model or memory of previous interactions. They operate based on predefined rules or simple decision-making processes.
   - **Example:** A thermostat adjusting the temperature based on current room conditions, or a basic chatbot that responds to keywords.
   - **Advantages:** Simple to design and efficient for straightforward tasks that do not require long-term planning or complex reasoning.
   - **Limitations:** Cannot adapt to changing conditions or learn from past experiences.
2. **Deliberative Agents:**
   - **Characteristics:** Deliberative agents possess an internal model of the world that allows them to plan, reason, and make decisions. They maintain memory and use algorithms such as search trees or planning systems to evaluate different actions.
   - **Example:** A self-driving car that not only reacts to immediate traffic signals but also plans its route based on maps, traffic conditions, and predicted future events.
   - **Advantages:** Can handle complex tasks that require foresight and decision-making over extended periods.
   - **Limitations:** Computationally expensive and may require significant time to make decisions, especially in dynamic or uncertain environments.
3. **Hybrid Agents:**
   - **Characteristics:** Hybrid agents combine elements of both reactive and deliberative approaches. These agents use reactive rules for immediate responses to stimuli while also employing deliberative planning for more complex decision-making.

- Example: A robotic vacuum that uses reactive behavior to avoid obstacles and follow simple patterns while planning an efficient path through the room.
- Advantages: Balances the speed and simplicity of reactive agents with the flexibility and adaptability of deliberative agents.
- Limitations: Designing hybrid agents can be more complex due to the need to combine different methods.

2. Agent Architectures

The architecture of an AI agent defines how its components are structured and how they interact to perform tasks. There are two main types of agent architectures: symbolic and subsymbolic.

Symbolic vs. Subsymbolic Agents

1. **Symbolic Agents (Good Old-Fashioned AI - GOFAI):**
   - **Characteristics:** Symbolic agents represent knowledge explicitly through symbols and use formal logic or rule-based systems to reason about the world. These agents rely on predefined knowledge and are often designed to emulate human reasoning.
   - **Example:** A chess-playing AI that uses a set of rules to evaluate different moves and select the best one based on the current state of the game.
   - **Strengths:** Well-suited for tasks that require explicit reasoning, such as logical deduction and rule-based problem-solving.
   - **Weaknesses:** Symbolic agents struggle with ambiguity, uncertainty, and learning from experience, making them less effective for complex or dynamic environments.
2. **Subsymbolic Agents (Connectionist AI):**
   - **Characteristics:** Subsymbolic agents use neural networks, genetic algorithms, or other machine learning methods to learn from data. These agents do not explicitly represent knowledge but instead learn patterns, representations, and strategies from training data.
   - **Example:** A neural network-based agent used for image recognition that learns to classify images based on patterns it detects in the training data.

- o **Strengths:** Capable of handling large amounts of unstructured data and learning from experience, making them suitable for tasks like image recognition, speech processing, and natural language understanding.
- o **Weaknesses:** Lack of interpretability and transparency, and difficulty in ensuring that the agent's behavior aligns with specific rules or intentions.

Modular Architectures

Modular architectures are designed to separate different components of an agent into distinct modules that each perform a specific function. This approach offers several benefits:

1. **Separation of Concerns:** Different aspects of the agent's functionality, such as perception, reasoning, and action, are handled by separate modules. This makes it easier to update and modify individual components without affecting the entire system.
2. **Flexibility:** New modules can be added or existing ones modified without redesigning the entire agent, making the architecture highly adaptable to changing requirements.
3. **Examples of Modular Architectures:**
   - o **Perception Module:** This module processes sensor data to interpret the environment.
   - o **Reasoning Module:** This module processes the data from the perception module and makes decisions.
   - o **Action Module:** Based on the reasoning, this module executes actions, such as controlling a robot's movement or generating a response in a chatbot.

3. Intelligence and Autonomy

AI agents vary in terms of their **intelligence** (the ability to reason, understand, and learn) and **autonomy** (the degree to which the agent can operate independently). Understanding these aspects is crucial for designing agents that can perform tasks effectively and adapt to new situations.

Levels of Autonomy in Agents

The autonomy of an AI agent can be broken down into several levels:

1. **Fully Autonomous Agents:**

o These agents are capable of performing tasks without human intervention. They make decisions, learn from their environment, and take actions based on their goals. Examples include autonomous vehicles and industrial robots.

2. **Semi-Autonomous Agents:**
   o Semi-autonomous agents may require human guidance or oversight for certain tasks. For example, an AI-powered drone might autonomously navigate but require human input for complex decision-making in certain environments.

3. **Human-Assisted Agents:**
   o These agents rely on human input for decision-making. A virtual assistant like Siri or Google Assistant may function autonomously for simple tasks, but for more complex inquiries or actions, it may request confirmation or further input from the user.

Decision-Making Processes

The decision-making process in an AI agent typically follows these steps:

1. **Perception:** The agent gathers data from the environment using sensors.
2. **Interpretation:** The agent processes the data to understand the context and relevance of the information.
3. **Decision-Making:** The agent selects an appropriate action based on its goals, available knowledge, and current situation.
4. **Action:** The agent takes action in the environment, whether it's moving a robotic arm or generating a response in a chat window.

AI agents may use a variety of decision-making models, including:

- **Rule-Based Systems:** Simple systems that make decisions based on predefined rules.
- **Machine Learning Models:** Models that learn from data and improve over time (e.g., reinforcement learning, supervised learning).
- **Planning Algorithms:** These agents reason about the future by creating a sequence of actions to achieve a goal, often using search algorithms or optimization techniques.

4. The Role of AI Agents in Modern Ecosystems

AI agents are an essential component of modern technological ecosystems, playing a critical role in a wide range of applications. They are integrated with other technologies like the **Internet of Things (IoT)** and **robotics** to create more intelligent, autonomous systems that can operate efficiently in real-world environments.

Integration with IoT, Robotics, and Other Technologies

1. **IoT and AI Agents:**
   - AI agents are increasingly integrated with IoT devices, enabling smart cities, homes, and industrial applications. For instance, AI agents can be used to monitor and control smart devices, like thermostats, lights, and security cameras, based on the data provided by sensors in the IoT ecosystem.
2. **Robotics and AI Agents:**
   - AI agents in robotics enable robots to perform autonomous tasks such as navigation, object manipulation, and human-robot interaction. In industrial settings, robots can autonomously assemble products, inspect machinery, or deliver goods without human intervention.
3. **Other Technologies:**
   - AI agents are also integrated into cloud computing, autonomous vehicles, and digital assistants. They enable systems to interact seamlessly with humans, learn from their interactions, and improve their functionality over time.

Impact on Various Industries

AI agents are transforming industries by automating complex tasks, improving efficiency, and enhancing decision-making. Key impacts include:

1. **Healthcare:** AI agents can assist doctors with diagnoses, monitor patient conditions, and provide personalized treatment recommendations.
2. **Finance:** AI agents are used in fraud detection, algorithmic trading, and customer service to improve decision-making and automate repetitive tasks.
3. **Customer Service:** Chatbots and virtual assistants are providing 24/7 customer support, handling queries, troubleshooting, and completing transactions.

4. **Manufacturing:** Autonomous robots and AI systems are optimizing production lines, reducing waste, and increasing productivity.
5. **Retail:** AI-powered recommendation systems are personalizing shopping experiences, improving inventory management, and enhancing customer engagement.

In summary, AI agents represent a broad field of intelligent systems capable of perceiving, reasoning, and acting autonomously in complex environments. By understanding their characteristics, architectures, levels of autonomy, and the role they play in modern ecosystems, we gain insight into how they can be used to solve real-world problems and drive innovation across industries.

Chapter 4: Planning and Designing LLM Agents

In this chapter, we will explore the critical steps involved in planning and designing Large Language Model (LLM) Agents. This process involves defining objectives, creating system architectures, selecting the appropriate tools and frameworks, and ensuring that the system is scalable and flexible to meet future demands. This chapter will guide you through each of these steps, providing clear, actionable insights that will help you design robust and effective LLM Agents.

1. Defining Objectives and Use Cases

Identifying Problems to Solve

The first step in designing any AI system, including LLM agents, is to clearly define the problem you are trying to solve. LLM agents can be deployed in a variety of settings, each with its own challenges. Identifying the core problem ensures that the solution you design is targeted and effective.

Here are the key steps to identifying the problems LLM agents can solve:

1. **Understand the Stakeholder Needs**:
   - Start by gathering information from the stakeholders who will use the LLM agent. This could include business owners, end-users, or subject matter experts.
   - For example, in a customer service application, the problem to solve could be improving response time, automating repetitive tasks, or providing more accurate responses to customer queries.
2. **Conduct a Needs Analysis**:
   - Analyze existing systems and identify gaps in functionality or performance. For example, if you're developing a virtual assistant for a medical application, identify what tasks current systems are unable to handle or could handle more efficiently.
3. **Define the Problem in Specific Terms**:
   - Clearly state what the agent should achieve. A well-defined problem might be something like, "The agent must answer customer queries related to product features and availability."

Mapping Requirements to Capabilities

Once the problem is identified, you need to translate it into functional requirements that the LLM agent must meet. This involves matching the problem with the capabilities of the LLM agent. Each LLM agent will have certain features and abilities based on the language model it uses, and these should align with the problem you are solving.

Example:

- **Problem:** Improve customer support by automating FAQs.
- **Requirements:**
    - The LLM agent must handle customer queries about product features, availability, shipping policies, and troubleshooting.
    - It should provide answers with high accuracy and in natural language, mimicking human customer support.

Mapping to LLM Capabilities:

- The agent will need a large corpus of domain-specific knowledge (which the LLM can be trained or fine-tuned on).
- It should be capable of interpreting a variety of question types (fact-based, conversational, etc.) using NLP techniques.

By systematically mapping the problem to LLM functionalities, you ensure that the agent will be capable of fulfilling its intended role effectively.

---

2. System Architecture Design

System architecture refers to the high-level design of the LLM agent and how its components interact. Designing a clear and robust system architecture is crucial for ensuring that the LLM agent can efficiently perform its tasks, scale when necessary, and be easily maintained.

High-Level Architecture Diagrams

The first step in designing the system architecture is to create high-level diagrams that illustrate how the LLM agent interacts with other components. These diagrams provide a visual understanding of how data flows through the system and the major building blocks.

Example of a High-Level Architecture for a Customer Support LLM Agent:

1. **User Input Interface**:
   o This could be a chat interface or voice recognition system. The user interacts with the agent through a web-based interface, mobile app, or smart device.
2. **Natural Language Processing (NLP) Component**:
   o This is the core of the LLM agent where the input is processed. The LLM processes the input and uses context and training data to generate an appropriate response.
3. **External Data Access Layer**:
   o For some use cases, the LLM agent may need to access external data such as product catalogs, user databases, or knowledge bases. This component ensures that the LLM can retrieve the most up-to-date information when generating responses.
4. **Decision-Making Module**:
   o Based on the input and external data, the LLM agent may need to make decisions. This component integrates logic and reasoning based on predefined rules or models (such as reinforcement learning or decision trees).
5. **Response Generation**:
   o This is where the output (response) is generated. The NLP model here utilizes the learned language patterns and relevant information to create a response. This may include performing actions like issuing a ticket, generating a document, or simply providing information.
6. **User Feedback/Monitoring**:
   o This component tracks the success or failure of the agent's actions and allows the system to be monitored for performance metrics. Feedback can be gathered to further refine the system.

(Note: This diagram can be added later as an example or flowchart.)

Component Interaction and Data Flow

Once the high-level architecture is established, it's essential to define how these components interact with each other. Understanding data flow between components is key to ensuring the system operates efficiently. Below is an example of how data might flow in a customer support LLM agent:

1. **User sends a query** via the chat interface (e.g., "What is the return policy for shoes?").
2. **NLP component processes** the query using pre-trained models and detects the user's intent (e.g., return policy).
3. **External data access layer** retrieves the relevant return policy data from a product database.
4. **Decision-making module** confirms that the query is understood and can generate a response.
5. **LLM generates a natural language response** ("Our return policy for shoes allows returns within 30 days of purchase with a receipt.").
6. **The response is sent back to the user** via the chat interface.
7. **User feedback** is recorded to monitor satisfaction and guide improvements.

---

3. Selecting Tools and Frameworks

Choosing the right tools and frameworks is crucial when building LLM agents. These tools provide the underlying infrastructure for processing data, training models, and deploying agents in real-world applications.

Overview of Popular AI Frameworks (TensorFlow, PyTorch, etc.)

Two of the most popular frameworks for building AI models, including LLMs, are **TensorFlow** and **PyTorch**. Both frameworks are widely used in the AI community, and understanding their differences is key to selecting the right one for your LLM agent.

1. **TensorFlow**:
   - **Pros**:
     - Extensive support for both research and production environments.
     - Good for large-scale machine learning tasks with strong scalability.
     - TensorFlow Serving provides an efficient way to deploy models into production.
   - **Cons**:

- TensorFlow's syntax can be more complex and less intuitive for beginners.

Example (TensorFlow for Training an LLM):

```
import tensorflow as tf

# Load pre-trained model and tokenizer
model = tf.keras.models.load_model("llm_model.h5")

# Sample input text
input_text = "How do I return a product?"

# Tokenize and predict the output
tokenizer = tf.keras.preprocessing.text.Tokenizer()
tokenized_input =
tokenizer.texts_to_sequences([input_text])
prediction = model.predict(tokenized_input)
print(prediction)
```

2. **PyTorch:**
   - **Pros:**
     - Easier to learn, especially for research and prototyping.
     - Highly flexible and dynamic (uses dynamic computation graphs).
     - Excellent support for GPU acceleration.
   - **Cons:**
     - Less optimized for deployment compared to TensorFlow (though this is changing).

Example (PyTorch for Training an LLM):

```
import torch
from transformers import GPT2LMHeadModel, GPT2Tokenizer

# Load pre-trained model
model = GPT2LMHeadModel.from_pretrained('gpt2')
tokenizer = GPT2Tokenizer.from_pretrained('gpt2')

# Encode the input text
input_text = "How do I return a product?"
inputs = tokenizer(input_text, return_tensors="pt")

# Generate response
outputs = model.generate(inputs["input_ids"],
max_length=50)
```

```
print(tokenizer.decode(outputs[0],
skip_special_tokens=True))
```

LLM-Specific Tools and Libraries

1. **Hugging Face Transformers**:
   - Hugging Face provides pre-trained models for various NLP tasks, including LLMs. It is one of the most widely used libraries for working with LLMs and provides an easy-to-use API for accessing and fine-tuning models like GPT-3, BERT, and T5.
2. **OpenAI GPT-3 API**:
   - For those who want to avoid the complexity of training their own LLM, OpenAI offers an API to interact with GPT-3. This API is ideal for applications that require powerful language generation but don't require custom model training.
3. **SpaCy**:
   - SpaCy is another powerful library for NLP, but it is more lightweight compared to Hugging Face and TensorFlow. It is best used for tasks like tokenization, part-of-speech tagging, and named entity recognition (NER).

---

4. Scalability and Flexibility Considerations

When designing an LLM agent, scalability and flexibility are crucial factors that ensure the system can handle growing data and adapt to new requirements over time.

Designing for Scalability

1. **Horizontal Scaling**:
   - In horizontal scaling, you increase the number of machines or processors to handle larger loads. For example, an LLM agent deployed in the cloud might use multiple server instances to process requests simultaneously, ensuring quick response times even during high traffic periods.
2. **Distributed Training**:
   - Large models like GPT-3 require significant computational resources. Using **distributed training** across multiple GPUs

or TPUs ensures that the model can be trained efficiently, even with massive datasets.

3. **Cloud Infrastructure**:
    o Leveraging cloud services like AWS, Google Cloud, or Azure can help in scaling the agent's infrastructure. Cloud services provide elastic computing resources that can scale up or down based on demand, making them a cost-effective solution for large-scale systems.

Ensuring System Flexibility and Modularity

1. **Modular Design**:
    o To ensure long-term maintainability and adaptability, the system should be designed with modular components. This allows for easy updates, replacements, or enhancements without disrupting the entire system.
2. **Microservices Architecture**:
    o Microservices allow each part of the LLM agent (such as the NLP module, data retrieval system, and decision-making engine) to function independently. This makes it easier to maintain, scale, and update specific components without affecting the rest of the system.
3. **Adaptability to New Models and Features**:
    o As AI models evolve and new features are introduced, the system should be designed to accommodate these changes with minimal effort. This might involve setting up an abstraction layer that can easily integrate new models or data sources.

Designing and building LLM agents requires a deep understanding of the problem to be solved, the architecture of the system, and the tools available to build and deploy these agents. By defining clear objectives, designing flexible and scalable systems, and selecting the right frameworks, you can create powerful, efficient, and adaptable LLM agents that can handle a wide range of tasks in various industries.

Chapter 5: Technical Integration of LLMs into Agent Frameworks

Integrating Large Language Models (LLMs) into agent frameworks is a crucial step in building functional and scalable AI systems. Whether you're utilizing pre-existing APIs or developing custom interfaces, understanding how to integrate LLMs with other systems and manage data efficiently is fundamental to building effective and secure agents. This chapter will cover the technical integration aspects, including APIs and interfaces, middleware and interoperability, data management, and security and privacy considerations.

1. APIs and Interfaces

Utilizing Existing APIs (OpenAI, Hugging Face, etc.)

APIs provide an easy way to interact with pre-trained LLMs without the need to develop and train models from scratch. Using existing APIs, such as **OpenAI's GPT-3 API** or **Hugging Face's Transformers**, allows you to quickly incorporate state-of-the-art LLM capabilities into your agent framework.

OpenAI GPT-3 API

OpenAI offers an API for interacting with GPT-3, one of the most powerful language models available today. By using this API, you can easily integrate natural language understanding and generation into your agent.

Example: Using OpenAI API for Text Generation

```
import openai

# Initialize OpenAI API
openai.api_key = 'your-api-key-here'

# Make a request to the API
response = openai.Completion.create(
  engine="text-davinci-003",  # GPT-3 model
  prompt="What are the benefits of using renewable energy?",
  max_tokens=100
)
```

```
# Display the response
print(response.choices[0].text.strip())
```

In this example:

- The `openai.Completion.create()` function makes a request to the GPT-3 API.
- The `prompt` parameter contains the input text that the model will process.
- `max_tokens` defines the maximum length of the response.

By utilizing such APIs, your agent can handle tasks like question answering, text generation, and more, without the need to handle the complexities of model training and infrastructure management.

Hugging Face API

Hugging Face provides a wide range of pre-trained models for natural language processing (NLP) tasks, including text generation, summarization, translation, and more. You can use their `transformers` library to easily access these models.

Example: Using Hugging Face's Transformers for Text Generation

```python
from transformers import GPT2LMHeadModel, GPT2Tokenizer

# Load pre-trained GPT-2 model and tokenizer
model = GPT2LMHeadModel.from_pretrained('gpt2')
tokenizer = GPT2Tokenizer.from_pretrained('gpt2')

# Encode input text
input_text = "How does machine learning impact business?"
inputs = tokenizer(input_text, return_tensors="pt")

# Generate output text
outputs = model.generate(inputs["input_ids"], max_length=50)
print(tokenizer.decode(outputs[0], skip_special_tokens=True))
```

This example uses Hugging Face's API to load a pre-trained GPT-2 model and generate a text response based on the input prompt.

Building Custom Interfaces

While existing APIs like OpenAI and Hugging Face provide easy-to-use solutions, there are cases where building a **custom interface** to interact with your LLM may be necessary. Custom interfaces allow for more flexibility and control over how the agent processes inputs and generates outputs.

Custom interfaces typically involve:

- **RESTful APIs**: Designing your own APIs that serve as communication interfaces between the LLM model and other systems.
- **WebSockets**: For real-time applications, WebSockets can allow for continuous, low-latency communication with the agent.
- **Custom Input/Output Processing**: You can preprocess input data or post-process the output to fit specific use cases, such as formatting responses, filtering content, or mapping outputs to specific actions.

Example: A Simple RESTful API for LLM Interaction

Using **Flask**, a lightweight Python web framework, you can create a simple API to serve your LLM agent.

```python
from flask import Flask, request, jsonify
from transformers import GPT2LMHeadModel, GPT2Tokenizer

app = Flask(__name__)

# Load pre-trained GPT-2 model
model = GPT2LMHeadModel.from_pretrained('gpt2')
tokenizer = GPT2Tokenizer.from_pretrained('gpt2')

@app.route('/generate', methods=['POST'])
def generate_text():
    input_text = request.json['input_text']
    inputs = tokenizer(input_text, return_tensors="pt")
    outputs = model.generate(inputs["input_ids"],
max_length=50)
    generated_text = tokenizer.decode(outputs[0],
skip_special_tokens=True)
    return jsonify({'generated_text': generated_text})

if __name__ == '__main__':
    app.run(debug=True)
```

In this example, the API listens for a POST request with the input text and returns the generated text from the LLM.

---

2. Middleware and Interoperability

Integrating an LLM agent into an existing ecosystem often requires connecting it with other systems, such as databases, third-party services, or sensor networks. **Middleware** is the software that enables this communication, providing the necessary functionality for data exchange and interaction.

Connecting LLMs with Other Systems

Middleware can help in connecting LLMs with external systems, such as:

- **Databases**: Retrieving and storing data that is relevant to the agent's tasks. For example, an LLM agent in a customer support application may need to access a product database to answer queries about stock availability.
- **APIs**: Interfacing with external APIs to provide additional data. For example, an LLM agent may call an external weather API to generate location-specific weather reports.

Data Exchange Protocols

Middleware systems often rely on data exchange protocols for communication between components. The most common protocols used in AI agent systems are:

- **HTTP/REST**: Used for web services and APIs, allowing agents to interact with web servers and databases.
- **WebSockets**: Allows for full-duplex communication channels between clients and servers, useful for real-time interactions.
- **Message Queues (e.g., RabbitMQ, Kafka)**: Used for asynchronous communication between systems, enabling decoupled architectures where agents can handle requests at their own pace.

Example: Middleware Using HTTP and WebSocket

```
import requests
```

```
# Example: Using REST API for Data Retrieval
response = requests.get("https://api.example.com/data")
data = response.json()

# Example: WebSocket Communication for Real-Time Interaction
import websocket

def on_message(ws, message):
    print(f"Received message: {message}")

ws = websocket.WebSocketApp("ws://example.com/socket",
on_message=on_message)
ws.run_forever()
```

In this example:

- A REST API request is made to retrieve data from an external service.
- WebSockets are used to listen for real-time messages.

3. Data Management and Storage

Handling data effectively is crucial when integrating LLMs into agent frameworks. LLMs often require large datasets for training and inference, so efficient data management and storage solutions are essential.

Handling Large Datasets

LLMs require vast amounts of text data for training and fine-tuning. Proper data management ensures that data is processed efficiently and available when needed.

- **Data Storage**:
  - For training data, large-scale storage solutions such as cloud storage (Amazon S3, Google Cloud Storage) or distributed file systems (HDFS) can be used.
  - For smaller-scale applications, traditional relational or NoSQL databases (MySQL, MongoDB) can store user queries and agent responses.
- **Data Preprocessing**:

o Preprocessing large datasets involves cleaning and tokenizing the data, ensuring that it is in a suitable format for the LLM.

Example: Storing Processed Data in MongoDB

```
from pymongo import MongoClient

# Connect to MongoDB
client = MongoClient('mongodb://localhost:27017/')
db = client['llm_agents']
collection = db['queries']

# Save processed data
data = {'query': 'How do I return a product?', 'response':
'Return within 30 days with a receipt.'}
collection.insert_one(data)
```

Efficient Data Retrieval and Processing

Efficient retrieval of data from databases is essential for performance, especially in real-time systems. Data indexing and caching mechanisms can speed up data access.

- **Indexing**: Indexing can make database queries faster by allowing the database to locate records more quickly.
- **Caching**: Frequently accessed data can be stored in a cache (e.g., Redis), reducing the need to access the database every time a request is made.

---

4. Security and Privacy

When building LLM-based agents, ensuring that sensitive data is protected is a critical concern. This section discusses strategies for safeguarding user data and ensuring secure communication channels.

Protecting Sensitive Data

LLMs often process sensitive user information, including personal details, payment information, and health data. Protecting this data requires implementing encryption and anonymization techniques.

- **Encryption**: Encrypt sensitive data both at rest (when stored) and in transit (during transmission). Techniques such as **AES (Advanced Encryption Standard)** can be used to encrypt data.
- **Data Anonymization**: In cases where data is processed for training purposes, anonymizing the data helps mitigate privacy concerns. For example, personal identifiers can be removed or replaced with random identifiers.

Example: Encrypting Data in Transit with HTTPS

```
import requests

# Make an HTTPS request (encrypted communication)
response = requests.get("https://secure-
api.example.com/data")
```

Implementing Secure Communication Channels

When an LLM agent communicates with external systems or users, it's essential to ensure that the communication is secure. This includes:

- **HTTPS**: Using HTTPS to ensure data is encrypted during transmission.
- **OAuth 2.0**: For authentication, especially when connecting to external APIs, OAuth 2.0 provides a secure way to grant limited access to resources without exposing credentials.

Example: Implementing OAuth Authentication

```
import requests
from requests.auth import OAuth2

# OAuth2 credentials
token = 'your_oauth_token_here'

# Secure API request
response = requests.get("https://api.example.com/data",
auth=OAuth2(token))
```

Integrating LLMs into agent frameworks involves several key steps, including utilizing APIs, connecting with other systems through middleware, managing large datasets efficiently, and ensuring robust security practices. By understanding these aspects, you can build scalable, flexible, and secure

LLM-based agents that can operate effectively across various domains. These integration techniques lay the foundation for creating intelligent agents capable of handling complex tasks in dynamic environments.

Chapter 6: Development Process for LLM Agents

Building a Large Language Model (LLM) Agent involves a well-structured development process that ensures the system operates effectively and efficiently. From setting up the development environment to implementing core functionalities and integrating with external services, this chapter will walk you through the necessary steps to develop a robust LLM agent. We will cover hardware and software requirements, best coding practices, key functional components, and integration strategies to make sure your agent performs optimally in real-world scenarios.

1. Setting Up the Development Environment

The development environment is the foundation for any AI project. It defines the hardware and software used to build, train, and deploy LLM agents. Having the right setup ensures smooth operations, faster iteration cycles, and optimized performance.

Hardware and Software Requirements

Hardware Requirements:

1. **CPU/GPU Requirements**:
   - LLMs, especially large models like GPT-3 or T5, require substantial computing power. **Graphics Processing Units (GPUs)** are essential for training and fine-tuning models. They significantly accelerate matrix computations, a key part of deep learning.
   - For smaller LLMs, a **high-performance CPU** might suffice, but for large-scale models, **NVIDIA GPUs** with CUDA support (e.g., Tesla V100, A100, or RTX 3080) are often used.
   - **TPUs** (Tensor Processing Units) offered by Google Cloud are also an excellent alternative for large-scale training tasks.
2. **Memory (RAM)**:
   - Large models can consume a lot of memory, so having sufficient **RAM** is crucial for smooth training and inference. At least **16 GB of RAM** is recommended for smaller models, but for large-scale LLMs, **64 GB or more** is ideal.

3. **Storage**:
   - ○ LLM models require **several terabytes of storage** for datasets and checkpoints, especially if fine-tuning or training models on custom data. Using **SSD storage** will ensure faster data access speeds.
   - ○ Cloud storage options such as **Amazon S3** or **Google Cloud Storage** are highly recommended for handling large datasets.

Software Requirements:

1. **Operating System**:
   - ○ Most AI development work is performed on **Linux-based operating systems** such as Ubuntu due to the stability and support for deep learning frameworks. However, **Windows** and **macOS** can also be used with proper configurations.
2. **Python**:
   - ○ Python is the primary programming language for most AI and LLM projects. Install Python 3.x, and ensure that it's the correct version for the dependencies you plan to use.
3. **AI Frameworks**:
   - ○ **TensorFlow** and **PyTorch** are the two most commonly used deep learning frameworks. These frameworks provide tools for training, fine-tuning, and deploying models.
4. **Docker**:
   - ○ Using **Docker** to containerize your development environment ensures that your LLM agent can be easily shared and deployed across different systems without the worry of compatibility issues.

Development Tools and IDEs

To streamline the development process, selecting the right development tools and integrated development environments (IDEs) is crucial.

1. **IDE/Editor**:
   - ○ **VS Code**: A popular, lightweight code editor with excellent support for Python and various plugins that help with debugging, code formatting, and Git integration.
   - ○ **PyCharm**: A full-fledged IDE specifically designed for Python development. It comes with features like automatic code suggestions, debugging tools, and version control integration.

2. **Jupyter Notebooks**:
   - For interactive development, **Jupyter Notebooks** is ideal. It allows you to write and execute code in a single document, making it easier to test ideas and visualize outputs.
3. **Version Control**:
   - **Git** is a fundamental tool for managing source code and tracking changes. Coupled with **GitHub**, GitLab, or **Bitbucket**, it allows developers to collaborate and store code remotely, ensuring code integrity and version control.

---

2. Coding Best Practices

Writing clean and maintainable code is essential for the longevity and scalability of any software project, including LLM agents. Following industry best practices helps ensure that the code is easy to read, modify, and scale as the project grows.

Writing Clean and Maintainable Code

1. **Code Structure and Organization**:
   - Organize your code into **modules** and **functions** that perform specific tasks. Each function should ideally have a single responsibility.
   - For larger projects, structure your code into directories, such as `/models`, `/data`, `/utils`, and `/scripts`, to help maintain clarity and modularity.
2. **Naming Conventions**:
   - Follow **PEP 8**, the Python style guide, for consistent naming conventions and formatting. For example:
     - Use **snake_case** for variable and function names (e.g., `process_input`).
     - Use **CamelCase** for class names (e.g., `LanguageModel`).
     - Use descriptive names for variables, functions, and classes that clearly convey their purpose.
3. **Documentation**:
   - Comment your code and write **docstrings** for functions and classes. The docstrings should explain the purpose of the function, its parameters, and the expected return value.

Example of a Function with Documentation:

```python
def preprocess_text(text: str) -> str:
    """
    Preprocesses the input text by converting to
    lowercase and removing punctuation.

    Parameters:
    text (str): The input text to be processed.

    Returns:
    str: The cleaned and preprocessed text.
    """
    # Convert text to lowercase
    text = text.lower()
    # Remove punctuation
    text = ''.join([char for char in text if
char.isalnum() or char.isspace()])
    return text
```

4. **Error Handling**:
   o Use **try-except blocks** to catch potential errors and exceptions, providing a clear message when something goes wrong.

Example:

```python
try:
    # Attempting to open a file
    with open('data.txt', 'r') as file:
        data = file.read()
except FileNotFoundError:
    print("File not found. Please check the file
path.")
```

Version Control and Collaboration (Git, GitHub)

Version control is crucial when working on large-scale projects, especially when collaborating with other developers. **Git** allows you to track changes, revert to previous versions, and manage branches for features and bug fixes.

1. **Git Basics**:
   o **git init**: Initialize a Git repository in your project folder.
   o **git add** : Add changes to the staging area.
   o **git commit -m "message"**: Commit changes with a descriptive message.

- ○ **git push**: Push commits to a remote repository (e.g., GitHub).
2. **Collaboration**:
    - ○ **Branching**: Use branches to work on new features or fixes. For example, you can create a branch called `feature/response-generator` to develop a new feature related to generating responses.
    - ○ **Pull Requests (PRs)**: Once a feature is complete, create a pull request for review. This allows team members to provide feedback before merging the feature into the main branch.

---

3. Implementing Core Functionalities

The core functionalities of an LLM agent typically include **language understanding**, **generation**, and **context management**. This section will focus on these essential modules and how to implement them.

Language Understanding and Generation Modules

1. **Language Understanding**:
    - ○ Use **Natural Language Processing (NLP)** techniques to process and understand user inputs. This can include tasks such as **tokenization**, **part-of-speech tagging**, and **named entity recognition**.

    For example, using **spaCy** for NLP tasks:

```
import spacy
nlp = spacy.load('en_core_web_sm')

# Process the text
doc = nlp("I love programming with Python!")

# Extract named entities
for entity in doc.ents:
    print(f"Entity: {entity.text}, Label:
{entity.label_}")
```

2. **Text Generation**:
    - ○ To generate responses or perform tasks like translation, summarization, or content creation, you can use an LLM like GPT-3 or GPT-2 for text generation.

Example of Text Generation using Hugging Face's GPT-2:

```
from transformers import GPT2LMHeadModel, GPT2Tokenizer

model = GPT2LMHeadModel.from_pretrained('gpt2')
tokenizer = GPT2Tokenizer.from_pretrained('gpt2')

input_text = "Once upon a time"
inputs = tokenizer(input_text, return_tensors="pt")
outputs = model.generate(inputs["input_ids"],
max_length=100)
print(tokenizer.decode(outputs[0],
skip_special_tokens=True))
```

Context Management and Memory

For LLM agents that interact with users over multiple turns (e.g., in a conversation), it is crucial to maintain context to provide coherent responses. This involves managing a **conversation history** or **persistent memory** that the agent can reference when making decisions.

1. **Short-Term Context**:
    o   Keep a history of the conversation or recent interactions to generate context-aware responses.

   Example of maintaining conversation history:

```
conversation_history = []

def add_to_history(user_input, agent_response):
    conversation_history.append({'user': user_input,
'agent': agent_response})

# Adding new interactions
add_to_history("How's the weather?", "It's sunny
today!")
```

2. **Long-Term Memory**:
    o   For more advanced agents, you might want to integrate long-term memory, allowing the agent to remember facts about users or tasks over time. This can be achieved by storing information in a database or persistent storage system.

4. Integration with External Services

Integrating LLM agents with external services can significantly enhance their functionality. Whether it's retrieving real-time data or interacting with third-party APIs, integration is key to creating intelligent and useful agents.

APIs for Additional Data and Functionality

LLMs can access a variety of data sources via APIs, including databases, knowledge bases, or web services.

Example of integrating an external API to retrieve data:

```python
import requests

def get_weather(city):
    api_url =
f"http://api.weatherapi.com/v1/current.json?key=YOUR_API_KEY&
q={city}"
    response = requests.get(api_url)
    data = response.json()
    return data['current']['condition']['text']

weather = get_weather("New York")
print(f"The current weather in New York is: {weather}")
```

Real-Time Data Processing

For tasks like live customer support or real-time decision-making, real-time data processing is essential. This can be achieved using technologies like **WebSockets**, **Kafka**, or **RabbitMQ** to handle continuous streams of data.

Example of real-time data processing with WebSockets:

```python
import websocket

def on_message(ws, message):
    print(f"Received message: {message}")

ws = websocket.WebSocketApp("ws://example.com/socket",
on_message=on_message)
ws.run_forever()
```

In this chapter, we've covered the key aspects of developing an LLM agent, from setting up the development environment and following coding best practices to implementing core functionalities and integrating with external services. By following these guidelines, you can build robust, efficient, and scalable LLM agents capable of handling a wide range of tasks and integrating seamlessly with other systems. As you continue to develop LLM agents, remember that the foundation you lay here—through proper environment setup, clean code, and effective integrations—will enable you to create intelligent and reliable AI systems.

Chapter 7: Testing and Deployment of LLM Agents

Once you've designed and built your Large Language Model (LLM) agent, it's crucial to ensure that it functions as expected in a real-world environment. Testing and deployment are essential steps in this process, as they validate the agent's behavior, performance, and scalability. In this chapter, we will delve into the testing methodologies for LLM agents, performance evaluation techniques, deployment strategies, and the ongoing maintenance and updates required to keep the system running smoothly.

1. Testing Methodologies

Unit Testing, Integration Testing, and System Testing

Testing is a fundamental step in ensuring that your LLM agent performs correctly under various conditions. The most common types of testing are **unit testing**, **integration testing**, and **system testing**.

1. **Unit Testing**:
   - Unit tests focus on testing individual components or functions of your LLM agent to ensure that they work correctly in isolation. Each unit of code is tested independently to verify that it behaves as expected.
   - For example, you might write unit tests for your text processing functions, such as tokenization, sentiment analysis, or entity recognition.

   Example: Unit Test for Text Preprocessing Function:

```python
import unittest
from text_preprocessing import preprocess_text

class TestTextProcessing(unittest.TestCase):
    def test_lowercase_conversion(self):
        self.assertEqual(preprocess_text("HELLO"),
"hello")

    def test_remove_punctuation(self):
        self.assertEqual(preprocess_text("Hello,
world!"), "Hello world")
```

```
if __name__ == '__main__':
    unittest.main()
```

- o In this example, we have created a unit test for the
  `preprocess_text` function to check whether it converts text
  to lowercase and removes punctuation correctly.

2. **Integration Testing**:
   - o Integration tests focus on testing the interaction between
     different components of your LLM agent. After testing
     individual functions (unit tests), you need to ensure that these
     components work together seamlessly.
   - o For instance, integration tests might check how well the NLP
     module interacts with the data retrieval module to process a
     user's query and generate a response.

Example: Integration Test for LLM Response Generation:

```
import unittest
from llm_agent import generate_response
from external_data import get_product_info

class TestLLMAgent(unittest.TestCase):
    def test_generate_response_with_data(self):
        query = "What is the price of the laptop?"
        expected_response = "The price of the laptop is
$999."
        # Simulate external data fetching
        product_data = get_product_info("laptop")
        response = generate_response(query,
product_data)
        self.assertEqual(response, expected_response)

if __name__ == '__main__':
    unittest.main()
```

- o Here, we test how well the `generate_response` function
  interacts with the `get_product_info` function, ensuring the
  integration between the LLM and external data is smooth.

3. **System Testing**:
   - o System testing is a broader testing methodology that
     examines the entire LLM agent as a whole, ensuring that all
     parts of the system work together as expected. It includes both
     functional and non-functional testing and covers real-world
     use cases and edge cases.

- During system testing, you test how the agent performs under different conditions, such as varying input sizes, network latencies, or unexpected behaviors.

Example: System Test for Full LLM Agent Interaction:

```
import unittest
from llm_agent import process_user_query

class TestSystemIntegration(unittest.TestCase):
    def test_full_interaction(self):
        query = "Tell me about AI in healthcare."
        response = process_user_query(query)
        self.assertIn("AI in healthcare", response)
        self.assertNotEqual(response, "")

if __name__ == '__main__':
    unittest.main()
```

- This test evaluates the full interaction of the LLM agent, verifying that it processes the query and returns a valid, non-empty response.

Automated Testing Tools

Automating the testing process is essential for efficiency, especially when working with large and complex systems. There are several tools available for automating tests:

1. **PyTest**: PyTest is a popular Python testing framework that supports unit tests, integration tests, and system tests. It is known for its simple syntax and powerful features, such as fixtures and parameterized tests.
2. **Jest**: Jest is a testing framework commonly used for testing JavaScript applications. It is often used in web-based LLM agent systems for frontend and backend testing.
3. **Selenium**: Selenium is used for automating web-based applications. It allows you to simulate user interactions with a web interface, which is especially useful when testing LLM agents that operate within a web environment.

2. Performance Evaluation

Evaluating the performance of your LLM agent is critical to ensure that it meets the required standards for speed, scalability, and efficiency. This includes assessing both functional performance (correctness) and non-functional performance (speed, load, and stress).

Metrics for Assessing AI Agent Performance

When evaluating LLM agent performance, you should focus on the following metrics:

1. **Response Accuracy**:
    o   Accuracy measures how well the agent's responses align with the expected output. For LLM agents, accuracy often refers to how correctly the model generates or interprets responses to user inputs.

    Example: Accuracy Metric:

    ```
    def accuracy_metric(predicted_response,
    expected_response):
        return predicted_response.strip().lower() ==
    expected_response.strip().lower()

    # Test case
    predicted = "The answer is 42."
    expected = "The answer is 42."
    print(accuracy_metric(predicted, expected))  # Output:
    True
    ```

2. **Response Time**:
    o   This metric measures how long it takes for the agent to respond to a user query. Faster response times lead to better user experiences.
    o   For large models, response time can be a critical factor. Optimizing LLM response times through efficient code, model inference optimizations, and server infrastructure is essential.

3. **Throughput**:
    o   Throughput refers to how many queries or tasks the agent can handle per unit of time. It is especially relevant in real-time

systems where the agent must handle multiple simultaneous requests.

4. **Latency**:
   - o Latency measures the time delay between sending a request to the agent and receiving a response. Minimizing latency is crucial in real-time systems, such as conversational agents or chatbots.

Load Testing and Stress Testing

1. **Load Testing**:
   - o Load testing evaluates how well the LLM agent performs under a normal or expected load. For example, how does the system behave when handling 100, 1000, or 10,000 user requests simultaneously?
   - o Tools like **Apache JMeter** or **Locust** can simulate high volumes of user traffic and evaluate the system's ability to handle it.

Example: Load Test with Locust:

```
from locust import HttpUser, task, between

class LLMUser(HttpUser):
    wait_time = between(1, 2)

    @task
    def query_agent(self):
        self.client.post("/query", json={"text": "What
is AI?"})
```

2. **Stress Testing**:
   - o Stress testing involves testing the system under extreme conditions (e.g., 100,000 simultaneous requests) to determine its breaking point. This helps identify bottlenecks and areas for improvement in scaling the system.

Example: Stress Test with JMeter:

   - o Set up multiple threads to simulate many users simultaneously interacting with the LLM agent.

3. Deployment Strategies

Once testing is complete, the next step is deployment. This process involves setting up the agent in a production environment and ensuring that it is reliable, scalable, and secure.

Cloud-Based Deployment (AWS, Azure, Google Cloud)

Cloud-based deployment is the most common strategy for deploying LLM agents, as it offers scalability, flexibility, and powerful computational resources. Leading cloud providers include:

1. **Amazon Web Services (AWS)**:
   o AWS provides various services for deploying AI applications, such as **EC2** for compute power, **S3** for storage, and **Lambda** for serverless functions.
   o **AWS SageMaker** is a fully managed service for deploying machine learning models at scale.
2. **Microsoft Azure**:
   o Azure offers similar services to AWS, including **Azure Machine Learning** for model deployment, and **Azure Functions** for serverless computing.
3. **Google Cloud**:
   o Google Cloud offers **AI Platform** for training and deploying machine learning models, along with **Compute Engine** for scalable compute resources.

Example: Deploying an LLM Agent on AWS:

- Use **AWS SageMaker** to deploy the model as an endpoint that can handle real-time inference requests.

On-Premises Deployment Considerations

Some organizations prefer on-premises deployment due to data privacy concerns, regulatory requirements, or network isolation.

1. **Hardware Requirements**:
   o On-premises deployments require powerful servers with GPUs for model inference, such as **NVIDIA A100** or **V100** GPUs, which are commonly used for AI model deployment.
2. **Infrastructure Setup**:

- o Setting up a robust on-premises infrastructure with load balancing, failover mechanisms, and disaster recovery plans is crucial for high availability.

---

4. Maintenance and Updates

Maintaining and updating your LLM agent ensures that it remains effective, secure, and adaptable to changing requirements over time.

Continuous Integration/Continuous Deployment (CI/CD)

CI/CD is an essential part of modern software development, especially when dealing with AI models and applications that require frequent updates. The CI/CD pipeline automates testing, integration, and deployment, ensuring that new features or fixes are integrated and deployed quickly.

1. **CI Tools**:
   - o Tools like **Jenkins, GitHub Actions**, and **GitLab CI** automate the testing and integration process.
2. **CD Tools**:
   - o Tools like **Kubernetes, Docker**, and **AWS CodePipeline** can automate deployment to cloud platforms, ensuring smooth, efficient deployment processes.

Monitoring and Logging

Once deployed, it's essential to monitor the LLM agent to ensure it functions properly. This includes tracking performance metrics (e.g., response time, accuracy), monitoring for errors, and logging system activities.

1. **Monitoring Tools**:
   - o **Prometheus** and **Grafana** can be used to monitor system performance and generate real-time dashboards for tracking agent health.
2. **Logging Tools**:
   - o Use logging frameworks like **Log4j** or **Fluentd** to track agent activities, debug errors, and analyze interactions for future improvements.

Example: Logging LLM Responses:

```python
import logging

# Set up logging
logging.basicConfig(level=logging.INFO)

def log_response(user_query, response):
    logging.info(f"User query: {user_query} | Agent response:
{response}")

# Example usage
log_response("What is AI?", "AI is the simulation of human
intelligence in machines.")
```

Testing and deployment are vital steps in the development lifecycle of LLM agents. By rigorously testing your agent through unit, integration, and system tests, you can ensure that it meets the necessary quality standards. Performance evaluation through load and stress testing ensures that the agent can handle high traffic while maintaining low latency. Once the agent is tested, deployment strategies like cloud-based or on-premises solutions can be used to scale the agent's capabilities. Continuous integration and monitoring help keep the agent updated and performing optimally. Following these guidelines will help ensure that your LLM agent is not only functional but also scalable, secure, and efficient in real-world applications.

Chapter 8: Enhancing Intelligence in LLM Agents

In this chapter, we will dive deep into advanced techniques and strategies that can significantly enhance the intelligence and capabilities of Large Language Model (LLM) agents. By incorporating machine learning techniques, improving natural language processing (NLP) capabilities, and integrating multimodal inputs, we can make LLM agents not only more intelligent but also more versatile in their ability to understand and generate human-like responses. This chapter will cover:

- Machine learning techniques to improve decision-making and learning.
- Enhancements to natural language understanding and generation.
- Integration of multimodal inputs, including text, images, audio, and video.

1. Incorporating Machine Learning Techniques

Machine learning plays a crucial role in enhancing the intelligence of LLM agents. It allows them to adapt, learn from experience, and improve over time. Below, we explore key machine learning paradigms that can be used to optimize LLM agents.

Supervised vs. Unsupervised Learning

1. **Supervised Learning**:
    - **Definition**: In supervised learning, the agent is trained on labeled data. The model learns to map input data to the correct output based on the examples it has seen during training. The goal is to minimize the difference between predicted outputs and the actual labels (the target outputs).
    - **Applications**: Supervised learning is often used in tasks such as classification, regression, and text generation, where there is a clear, labeled dataset.

    Example: Training an LLM on a set of customer support conversations with labels like "Query" or "Response". The model learns to predict whether a piece of text is a customer query or the agent's response.

Code Example: Supervised Learning for Text Classification:

```
from sklearn.model_selection import train_test_split
from sklearn.naive_bayes import MultinomialNB
from sklearn.feature_extraction.text import
CountVectorizer

# Example dataset
texts = ["How can I return a product?", "What is the
shipping policy?", "How do I cancel an order?"]
labels = ['query', 'query', 'query']  # Labels for the
input texts

# Convert text to feature vectors
vectorizer = CountVectorizer()
X = vectorizer.fit_transform(texts)
y = labels

# Split the data into training and testing sets
X_train, X_test, y_train, y_test = train_test_split(X,
y, test_size=0.2)

# Train a classifier
clf = MultinomialNB()
clf.fit(X_train, y_train)

# Make predictions
predictions = clf.predict(X_test)
print(predictions)
```

2. **Unsupervised Learning**:
   - o **Definition**: Unsupervised learning involves training a model on data that has no labels or targets. The model identifies patterns and structures in the data, such as clusters or associations. It is particularly useful when labeled data is unavailable or scarce.
   - o **Applications**: Unsupervised learning is used for clustering, anomaly detection, dimensionality reduction, and more. In LLM agents, unsupervised techniques can help identify patterns or topics from a large corpus of text without the need for labeled examples.

Example: A topic modeling algorithm such as Latent Dirichlet Allocation (LDA) might be used to uncover topics in a large set of customer service dialogues, helping to automatically categorize interactions.

Code Example: Unsupervised Learning for Topic Modeling with LDA:

```
from sklearn.decomposition import
LatentDirichletAllocation
from sklearn.feature_extraction.text import
CountVectorizer

# Sample corpus of customer service dialogues
texts = ["I need to return a product.", "How do I track
my order?", "I want to cancel my order."]

# Vectorize the text data
vectorizer = CountVectorizer(stop_words='english')
X = vectorizer.fit_transform(texts)

# Apply LDA for topic modeling
lda = LatentDirichletAllocation(n_components=2,
random_state=42)
lda.fit(X)

# Display topics
for idx, topic in enumerate(lda.components_):
    print(f"Topic {idx}:")
    print([vectorizer.get_feature_names_out()[i] for i
in topic.argsort()[:-6 - 1:-1]])
```

Reinforcement Learning for Decision Making

Reinforcement Learning (RL) is a type of machine learning where an agent learns by interacting with its environment and receiving feedback in the form of rewards or penalties. In the context of LLM agents, RL can be applied to improve decision-making processes, especially when the agent needs to optimize its actions over time.

- **Goal**: The agent learns a policy to maximize cumulative rewards by taking actions in an environment. For example, an LLM agent might interact with users in a chatbot scenario, learning to maximize user satisfaction by making better decisions based on past interactions.

Code Example: Reinforcement Learning with Q-Learning

```
import numpy as np

# Q-table initialization (state-action value table)
q_table = np.zeros((5, 5))  # Assume 5 states and 5 possible
actions
```

```
# Hyperparameters
learning_rate = 0.1
discount_factor = 0.9
epsilon = 0.1  # Exploration vs. exploitation tradeoff

# Simple Q-learning algorithm for decision-making
def choose_action(state):
    if np.random.rand() < epsilon:
        return np.random.choice(5)  # Exploration
    else:
        return np.argmax(q_table[state])  # Exploitation

# Example interaction loop
for episode in range(1000):
    state = np.random.randint(0, 5)  # Random starting state
    action = choose_action(state)
    reward = np.random.rand()  # Simulated reward (between 0
and 1)

    # Update Q-table using the Q-learning equation
    next_state = (state + 1) % 5  # Transition to the next
state (simplified)
    q_table[state, action] = q_table[state, action] +
learning_rate * (reward + discount_factor *
np.max(q_table[next_state]) - q_table[state, action])

print("Q-Table after learning:")
print(q_table)
```

In this example, the RL agent learns to maximize its rewards through interaction with the environment by updating the Q-table based on the rewards it receives.

---

2. Natural Language Processing (NLP) Enhancements

Enhancing NLP capabilities within an LLM agent is essential for improving the agent's ability to understand and generate human language effectively. Below, we will explore key enhancements in semantic understanding and contextual awareness.

Semantic Understanding

Semantic understanding involves interpreting the meaning behind words, sentences, and entire passages. Enhancements in semantic understanding enable the LLM agent to grasp the underlying intent and context of user inputs.

- **Named Entity Recognition (NER)**: This technique helps the model identify and classify entities in text (e.g., person names, locations, organizations).
- **Word Sense Disambiguation (WSD)**: Helps the agent understand different meanings of a word based on context. For example, "bank" can mean a financial institution or the side of a river, depending on the context.

Example: Using spaCy for Named Entity Recognition (NER)

```python
import spacy

# Load pre-trained spaCy model
nlp = spacy.load("en_core_web_sm")

# Sample text
text = "Apple is planning to open a new store in San Francisco."

# Process the text
doc = nlp(text)

# Extract named entities
for entity in doc.ents:
    print(f"Entity: {entity.text}, Label: {entity.label_}")
```

Contextual Awareness and Coherence

Contextual awareness refers to the agent's ability to understand the context of a conversation or document, maintaining coherence across interactions. For LLMs, this involves the ability to track and reference prior interactions, keeping responses relevant and coherent.

1. **Contextual Embeddings**: Models like **BERT** and **GPT-3** use contextual embeddings to capture word meanings based on the surrounding words in a sentence or paragraph. This allows the LLM agent to understand polysemy and nuances in language.
2. **Attention Mechanisms**: Attention mechanisms, like the **self-attention** in Transformers, allow the model to focus on the most relevant parts of a sequence, maintaining coherence even in long conversations.

3. Multimodal Integration

Incorporating multimodal data (text, images, audio, and video) into LLM agents can significantly expand their capabilities, enabling them to process and generate content that is more aligned with human-like sensory processing.

Combining Text with Images, Audio, and Video

1. **Text and Image Integration**: By combining LLMs with **computer vision models** (e.g., CNNs, vision transformers), agents can interpret images and generate textual descriptions or responses based on visual input.

   Example: Using **CLIP** (Contrastive Language-Image Pretraining) to understand images and text together:

   ```
   from transformers import CLIPProcessor, CLIPModel

   model = CLIPModel.from_pretrained("openai/clip-vit-
   base-patch32")
   processor = CLIPProcessor.from_pretrained("openai/clip-
   vit-base-patch32")

   text = ["a photo of a cat"]
   image = Image.open("cat.jpg")

   inputs = processor(text=text, images=image,
   return_tensors="pt", padding=True)
   outputs = model(**inputs)
   logits_per_image = outputs.logits_per_image # this is
   the image-text similarity score
   ```

2. **Text and Audio Integration**: LLM agents can also integrate with **speech recognition models** (e.g., **Whisper, DeepSpeech**) to transcribe and respond to spoken language in real-time.

   Example: Speech-to-text conversion using **SpeechRecognition** library:

   ```
   import speech_recognition as sr

   recognizer = sr.Recognizer()
   ```

```
with sr.Microphone() as source:
    print("Listening for speech...")
    audio = recognizer.listen(source)

try:
    text = recognizer.recognize_google(audio)
    print("You said: " + text)
except sr.UnknownValueError:
    print("Sorry, I could not understand the audio.")
```

Applications of Multimodal LLM Agents

Multimodal LLM agents can be used in various applications, including:

1. **Healthcare**: LLM agents can analyze medical images (X-rays, MRIs) alongside text-based clinical data to assist in diagnosis and treatment planning.
2. **Education**: Multimodal agents can process and generate both textual and visual content, providing personalized learning experiences.
3. **Autonomous Vehicles**: In autonomous driving, LLM agents can combine sensor data, visual inputs, and text to navigate complex environments.

Enhancing the intelligence of LLM agents requires the integration of advanced machine learning techniques, improved NLP capabilities, and the ability to process multimodal data. By applying supervised and unsupervised learning, reinforcement learning,

and enhancing semantic understanding and contextual awareness, you can create more intelligent and adaptive LLM agents. Additionally, multimodal integration allows LLM agents to process and understand diverse types of data, improving their versatility in real-world applications. These advancements pave the way for building more powerful, human-like AI agents capable of handling complex, dynamic tasks across a wide range of industries.

Chapter 9: Autonomy and Decision-Making Algorithms

In this chapter, we explore the foundational concepts related to autonomy and decision-making in Large Language Model (LLM) agents. We will cover how these agents can make decisions independently, adapt to new situations, and follow ethical guidelines while making choices. Autonomy in AI is crucial for enabling intelligent behavior, as it allows agents to perform tasks with minimal human intervention. By understanding the different decision-making models and incorporating ethical considerations, we can design LLM agents that operate responsibly and efficiently. This chapter covers the following topics:

- Autonomous behavior models, including goal-oriented behavior and self-learning.
- Decision-making frameworks, including rule-based systems, probabilistic models, and neural decision networks.
- Ethical decision-making, including incorporating ethical guidelines and balancing autonomy with human oversight.

1. Autonomous Behavior Models

Autonomy refers to the ability of an agent to perform tasks without human intervention. An autonomous agent should be able to make decisions based on its goals, the environment, and past experiences. Here, we explore two critical aspects of autonomous behavior: goal-oriented behavior and self-learning.

Goal-Oriented Behavior

Goal-oriented behavior is one of the fundamental characteristics of autonomous agents. These agents act based on predefined objectives and take actions that maximize the likelihood of achieving their goals.

1. **Goal Formulation**:
   - The agent must first identify a clear goal. For instance, in a customer service scenario, the goal might be to resolve a user's query by providing an accurate answer.
2. **Action Selection**:

- o Once the goal is established, the agent selects actions that move it closer to achieving that goal. For example, a chatbot might choose to gather additional context or ask clarifying questions to refine its response.
3. **Feedback Loops**:
   - o The agent continuously monitors its progress toward the goal and adjusts its actions accordingly. If a given action doesn't help achieve the goal, the agent may abandon that path and try a different one.
4. **Example**: A robot vacuum cleaner is an autonomous agent with the goal of cleaning a room. It navigates the room, detects obstacles, and adjusts its path based on its goal of covering the entire room while avoiding furniture.

Self-Learning and Adaptation

Self-learning agents are capable of improving their behavior over time based on past experiences. This adaptation allows them to refine their decision-making processes and better achieve their goals in future interactions.

1. **Reinforcement Learning (RL)**:
   - o Reinforcement learning is a popular approach to enable self-learning. The agent interacts with its environment, receives feedback in the form of rewards or penalties, and adjusts its behavior to maximize cumulative rewards.

   Example of RL in LLM Agents: An LLM agent in a customer service setting could learn to prioritize more urgent queries based on feedback from users about satisfaction levels.

2. **Exploration vs. Exploitation**:
   - o A key challenge in self-learning agents is the balance between exploration (trying new actions) and exploitation (choosing the best-known action). This balance is critical for agents to discover optimal solutions while avoiding repetitive behavior.

   Code Example: Simple Q-Learning for Goal-Oriented Behavior:

```
import numpy as np

# Initialize Q-table for Q-Learning
q_table = np.zeros((5, 5))  # Assume 5 states and 5
actions
```

```
# Hyperparameters
learning_rate = 0.1
discount_factor = 0.9
epsilon = 0.1  # Exploration rate

def choose_action(state):
    if np.random.rand() < epsilon:
        return np.random.choice(5)  # Exploration
    else:
        return np.argmax(q_table[state])  #
Exploitation

def update_q_table(state, action, reward, next_state):
    best_next_action = np.argmax(q_table[next_state])
    q_table[state, action] = q_table[state, action] +
learning_rate * (reward + discount_factor *
q_table[next_state, best_next_action] - q_table[state,
action])

# Simulate learning process
state = 0
action = choose_action(state)
reward = 1  # Simulated reward
next_state = 1  # Transition to the next state
update_q_table(state, action, reward, next_state)

print("Updated Q-Table:", q_table)
```

In this code, the agent learns by updating the Q-table based on the reward it receives from taking actions. Over time, it refines its behavior to optimize rewards.

---

2. Decision-Making Frameworks

Decision-making in LLM agents can be approached in various ways, depending on the complexity of the problem, the environment, and the objectives of the agent. The primary frameworks for decision-making include rule-based systems, probabilistic models, and neural decision networks.

Rule-Based Systems vs. Probabilistic Models

1. **Rule-Based Systems**:

- Rule-based systems make decisions based on predefined rules. These rules typically take the form of "if-then" statements. This approach works well when the decision-making process is well-understood and deterministic.

Example of a Rule-Based System:

- If the input is "I want to cancel my order," the agent might respond with "Please provide your order number."

Code Example: Simple Rule-Based Response System

```
def rule_based_agent(query):
    rules = {
        "cancel order": "Please provide your order
number.",
        "track order": "Please enter your tracking
number."
    }

    for key in rules:
        if key in query.lower():
            return rules[key]
    return "Sorry, I didn't understand your request."

# Example usage
query = "How can I cancel my order?"
print(rule_based_agent(query))  # Output: "Please
provide your order number."
```

2. **Probabilistic Models**:
   - Probabilistic models make decisions based on the likelihood of different outcomes. They use statistical methods to assess the probability of each action, and choose the one that maximizes expected utility.
   - **Bayesian Networks**: A powerful framework for decision-making under uncertainty, where the agent uses probability theory to update beliefs about the environment as new information arrives.

Example: A probabilistic model might be used to predict the most likely response to a customer inquiry, given historical data.

Code Example: Simple Bayesian Inference for Decision Making

```
import numpy as np

# Example: Decision probabilities for different actions
actions = ["track order", "cancel order", "return
product"]
probabilities = np.array([0.2, 0.5, 0.3])  #
Probabilities for each action

def choose_action(probabilities):
    return np.random.choice(actions, p=probabilities)

print("Chosen Action:", choose_action(probabilities))
```

Neural Decision Networks

Neural Decision Networks (NDNs) use neural networks to make decisions based on complex patterns in data. NDNs combine the flexibility of deep learning with decision-making tasks, enabling more sophisticated and adaptive behavior than rule-based or probabilistic systems.

1. **How NDNs Work**:
   - NDNs can be trained on large datasets to learn decision-making policies based on past experiences. These networks can integrate multiple inputs and consider complex relationships between them to generate outputs.
2. **Applications of Neural Decision Networks**:
   - **Autonomous Vehicles**: Deciding how to steer the vehicle based on real-time sensor data (e.g., cameras, LiDAR).
   - **Robotic Systems**: Making decisions about movement or task execution based on feedback from the environment.

Code Example: Simple Neural Network for Decision Making (Using PyTorch)

```
import torch
import torch.nn as nn
import torch.optim as optim

# Define a simple neural network for decision making
class DecisionNetwork(nn.Module):
    def __init__(self):
        super(DecisionNetwork, self).__init__()
        self.fc1 = nn.Linear(3, 64)  # 3 input features, 64
hidden units
        self.fc2 = nn.Linear(64, 3)  # 3 output actions
```

```python
def forward(self, x):
    x = torch.relu(self.fc1(x))
    x = self.fc2(x)
    return x

# Initialize network, loss function, and optimizer
model = DecisionNetwork()
criterion = nn.MSELoss()
optimizer = optim.Adam(model.parameters(), lr=0.001)

# Sample input (e.g., environment state)
input_data = torch.tensor([0.5, 0.1, 0.7],
dtype=torch.float32)

# Predict the action
output = model(input_data)
print("Action Scores:", output)
```

In this example, the neural network outputs a set of scores representing the desirability of different actions, which can then be used to select the best action based on the model's training.

---

3. Ethical Decision-Making

Ethical decision-making is one of the most critical aspects of autonomous LLM agents, especially as AI systems are being deployed in real-world scenarios where their actions can impact human lives. Incorporating ethical considerations into decision-making algorithms ensures that agents act responsibly, align with societal values, and avoid harmful behaviors.

Incorporating Ethical Guidelines

1. **Ethical Frameworks**:
   - Various ethical frameworks can be used to guide decision-making in autonomous agents. These include utilitarian approaches (maximizing overall happiness or well-being) and deontological approaches (following rules or duties).
2. **Ethical Constraints**:
   - Ethical guidelines can be encoded as rules or constraints that the agent must adhere to. For instance, an autonomous agent in healthcare should avoid making decisions that could harm patients or violate privacy.

3. **Example**: An autonomous healthcare assistant should prioritize patient safety above all else, even if this means forgoing efficiency or convenience.

Balancing Autonomy with Human Oversight

While autonomy is critical for efficiency, human oversight is necessary to ensure that the agent's decisions align with ethical principles and societal norms. A hybrid approach, where the agent can make decisions independently but human intervention is possible when needed, is ideal.

1. **Human-in-the-Loop**:
   o This approach ensures that the agent's decisions are reviewed or approved by a human operator, especially for high-stakes situations where ethical concerns are prominent.
2. **Transparency and Explainability**:
   o Providing explanations for an agent's decisions (Explainable AI, or XAI) can help human overseers understand the rationale behind decisions, making it easier to intervene if necessary.

Code Example: Ethical Decision-Making Framework (Simplified)

```
def ethical_decision_making(action_scores,
ethical_constraints):
    """
    Makes a decision by considering action scores and ethical
constraints.
    Ensures the action respects ethical guidelines.
    """
    for constraint in ethical_constraints:
        if constraint == "patient safety":
            # Reject any action that risks patient safety
            if action_scores["unsafe_action"] > 0.8:
                return "Action Rejected: Safety Concerns"

    # If all constraints are satisfied, return the best
action
    return max(action_scores, key=action_scores.get)

# Example action scores (representing desirability of
different actions)
action_scores = {"safe_action": 0.9, "unsafe_action": 0.7}

# Ethical constraints (e.g., patient safety priority)
ethical_constraints = ["patient safety"]
```

```
print(ethical_decision_making(action_scores,
ethical_constraints))
```

In this example, the decision-making algorithm ensures that actions that compromise patient safety are automatically rejected, prioritizing ethical considerations.

Autonomy and decision-making are central to the operation of LLM agents, allowing them to act intelligently in dynamic environments. By incorporating goal-oriented behavior, self-learning, and various decision-making frameworks (rule-based, probabilistic models, and neural decision networks), LLM agents can make decisions independently and adapt to new situations. Furthermore, integrating ethical guidelines and balancing autonomy with human oversight ensures that LLM agents act responsibly and in alignment with societal values. These advancements are crucial for deploying intelligent, ethical, and responsible LLM agents across diverse real-world applications.

Chapter 10: Performance Optimization Techniques

As Large Language Model (LLM) agents are deployed in increasingly demanding environments, ensuring that they run efficiently and effectively is critical. Performance optimization techniques not only improve the speed and responsiveness of the agent but also help manage resources like memory and computational power. This chapter will explore key performance optimization strategies, including enhancing speed and efficiency, managing resources, and ensuring scalability. By implementing these techniques, you can build LLM agents that are both high-performing and capable of handling large-scale tasks.

1. Speed and Efficiency Enhancements

Model Pruning and Quantization

1. **Model Pruning**:
   - **Definition**: Model pruning is the process of removing weights or neurons from a neural network that have little to no impact on the model's performance. The goal is to reduce the complexity of the model, leading to faster inference times without significantly affecting its accuracy.
   - **Benefits**: Pruning helps reduce the size of the model, which in turn decreases memory usage and computational costs. This is particularly useful for deploying models on resource-constrained devices.
   - **Types of Pruning**:
     - **Weight Pruning**: Removing individual weights from a network.
     - **Neuron Pruning**: Removing entire neurons or layers from the network.
     - **Structured Pruning**: Removing entire groups of parameters, such as filters in convolutional layers.

   Example: Weight Pruning with PyTorch:

```
import torch
import torch.nn.utils.prune as prune

# Define a simple neural network
```

```python
class SimpleModel(torch.nn.Module):
    def __init__(self):
        super(SimpleModel, self).__init__()
        self.fc = torch.nn.Linear(10, 10)

    def forward(self, x):
        return self.fc(x)

# Instantiate the model
model = SimpleModel()

# Apply pruning to the linear layer
prune.random_unstructured(model.fc, name="weight",
amount=0.2)

# Print the pruned weights
print(model.fc.weight)
```

- o In this example, `prune.random_unstructured()` prunes 20% of the weights from the linear layer of the model. This reduces the number of parameters, improving speed and efficiency during inference.

2. **Quantization**:
   - o **Definition**: Quantization is the process of reducing the precision of the numbers used to represent the model's weights and activations, typically from 32-bit floating point to 16-bit or even 8-bit integers. This reduces both the size of the model and the computation required for inference, without significantly losing accuracy.
   - o **Benefits**: Quantization is particularly effective in making models more efficient for deployment on hardware with limited resources, such as mobile devices or embedded systems.

Example: Quantization with PyTorch:

```python
import torch
from torch import quantization

# Define a simple model
model = torch.nn.Linear(10, 10)

# Convert the model to a quantized version
model = quantization.quantize_dynamic(model,
dtype=torch.qint8)

# Print the quantized model
```

```
print(model)
```

- o Here, `quantization.quantize_dynamic()` converts the model's weights to 8-bit integers, reducing its size and computation costs while maintaining similar performance.

Hardware Acceleration (GPUs, TPUs)

1. **Graphics Processing Units (GPUs)**:
   - o **Definition**: GPUs are specialized hardware designed for parallel processing, making them ideal for training and running large deep learning models. They significantly accelerate matrix operations, which are central to deep learning computations.
   - o **Benefits**: GPUs can handle the large-scale computations involved in LLM inference at high speeds, reducing latency and improving throughput. They are commonly used for both training and serving models.

   Example: Using GPU in PyTorch:

```
import torch

# Check if a GPU is available
device = torch.device("cuda" if
torch.cuda.is_available() else "cpu")

# Move model and data to the GPU
model = torch.nn.Linear(10, 10).to(device)
data = torch.randn(5, 10).to(device)

# Perform a forward pass on the GPU
output = model(data)
print(output)
```

   - o This code snippet demonstrates how to move both the model and input data to the GPU, significantly accelerating the computation compared to using a CPU.
2. **Tensor Processing Units (TPUs)**:
   - o **Definition**: TPUs are specialized hardware accelerators developed by Google, optimized for deep learning tasks. They are designed to perform tensor operations (multi-dimensional arrays) extremely efficiently.

- o **Benefits**: TPUs offer better performance than GPUs for certain types of deep learning workloads, particularly for large models and large datasets. They are available through cloud services like Google Cloud.

Example: Using TPUs with TensorFlow:

```
import tensorflow as tf

# Define a simple model
model = tf.keras.Sequential([
    tf.keras.layers.Dense(10, input_shape=(10,))
])

# Set up the TPU strategy
tpu_strategy = tf.distribute.TPUStrategy()

with tpu_strategy.scope():
    model.compile(optimizer='adam', loss='mse')

# Train the model
model.fit(x_train, y_train, epochs=10)
```

- o This code shows how to use TPUs with TensorFlow by wrapping the model and training process inside a TPU strategy.

---

2. Resource Management

Efficient resource management ensures that LLM agents utilize memory and computational resources optimally, reducing waste and improving overall performance. This is particularly important when deploying models in environments with limited resources.

Optimizing Memory Usage

1. **Memory Efficient Techniques**:
   - o **Gradient Checkpointing**: In deep learning models, saving intermediate results of forward passes can consume a lot of memory. Gradient checkpointing allows you to save memory by recalculating intermediate results during the backward pass, rather than storing them.

- o **Offloading**: Moving certain processes to secondary memory (like disk storage) when they are not immediately needed can help reduce memory pressure.
2. **Memory Profiling**:
   - o Tools like **PyTorch's memory profiler** or **TensorFlow Profiler** allow you to monitor memory usage during training and inference. By identifying memory bottlenecks, you can make informed decisions about model optimizations.

Example: Using PyTorch Memory Profiling:

```
import torch
from torch.utils import profiler

# Start profiling
with profiler.profile(record_shapes=True) as prof:
    model = torch.nn.Linear(10, 10)
    data = torch.randn(5, 10)
    output = model(data)

# Print memory usage and other details
print(prof.key_averages().table(sort_by="cpu_time_total"))
```

   - o This code uses the `profiler.profile()` function to monitor memory usage during the forward pass of a simple model.

Efficient Data Pipeline Design

1. **Data Preprocessing**:
   - o For LLMs, data preprocessing is a critical step. However, preprocessing large datasets can be resource-intensive. By offloading data preprocessing tasks to parallel processes or GPUs, you can reduce the overall time taken for training and inference.
2. **Data Augmentation**:
   - o Data augmentation techniques can help reduce the need for large amounts of data by artificially expanding the training dataset. This can be particularly useful when working with image or text data.
3. **Asynchronous Data Loading**:
   - o Asynchronous loading of data allows the training process to continue without waiting for the data to be fully loaded. Using

data generators or asynchronous queues can ensure that data is continuously fed to the model during training.

Example: Asynchronous Data Loading in PyTorch:

```python
from torch.utils.data import DataLoader

class MyDataset(torch.utils.data.Dataset):
    def __init__(self, data):
        self.data = data

    def __len__(self):
        return len(self.data)

    def __getitem__(self, idx):
        return self.data[idx]

# Create a DataLoader with asynchronous data loading
dataset = MyDataset(data)
dataloader = DataLoader(dataset, batch_size=32,
num_workers=4, pin_memory=True)

for batch in dataloader:
    process(batch)
```

o   In this example, `num_workers=4` allows for asynchronous data loading using multiple CPU threads.

---

3. Scalability Solutions

Scalability is the ability of an LLM agent to handle growing amounts of work or its potential to accommodate growth. As demand increases, the agent must be able to scale both vertically (using more powerful hardware) and horizontally (using more machines).

Distributed Computing

1. **Definition**: Distributed computing involves spreading computations across multiple machines to handle large workloads. This allows LLM agents to scale efficiently by distributing data processing and model inference across different nodes or clusters.
2. **Example: Distributed Training with PyTorch**:

- o PyTorch's **DistributedDataParallel** allows you to train models on multiple GPUs across different machines, speeding up the training process and enabling the use of very large datasets.

Code Example:

```
import torch
import torch.distributed as dist
from torch.nn.parallel import DistributedDataParallel
as DDP

dist.init_process_group(backend='nccl',
init_method='env://')

model = MyModel().to(device)
ddp_model = DDP(model)

# Distributed training loop
for data in data_loader:
    outputs = ddp_model(data)
    loss = compute_loss(outputs)
    loss.backward()
```

- o This code sets up distributed training across multiple GPUs using PyTorch's DDP module.

Load Balancing and Fault Tolerance

1. **Load Balancing**:
   - o Load balancing ensures that requests to the LLM agent are distributed evenly across multiple servers or instances, preventing any single server from becoming overwhelmed. This is essential for maintaining fast response times under high demand.
   - o **Cloud Load Balancers**: Many cloud platforms (AWS, Google Cloud, Azure) offer load balancers that can automatically distribute incoming traffic to multiple servers hosting the LLM agent.
2. **Fault Tolerance**:
   - o Fault tolerance ensures that the system remains operational even when some components fail. By using redundant systems and automatic failover mechanisms, you can ensure high availability and reliability for LLM agents.

Example: Using Kubernetes for Load Balancing and Fault Tolerance:

```
apiVersion: apps/v1
kind: Deployment
metadata:
  name: llm-agent
spec:
  replicas: 3  # Multiple instances for fault tolerance
and load balancing
  selector:
    matchLabels:
      app: llm-agent
  template:
    metadata:
      labels:
        app: llm-agent
    spec:
      containers:
      - name: llm-agent
        image: llm-agent-image
        ports:
        - containerPort: 8080
```

- o In this example, **Kubernetes** manages the deployment of three replicas of the LLM agent, providing both load balancing and fault tolerance.

In this chapter, we've explored several performance optimization techniques that are crucial for deploying high-performing LLM agents. These techniques include model pruning and quantization for speed and efficiency, hardware acceleration using GPUs and TPUs, and efficient resource management strategies. We also covered scalability solutions such as distributed computing and load balancing to ensure that LLM agents can scale effectively as demand grows. By applying these optimization strategies, you can enhance the performance, scalability, and efficiency of your LLM agents, making them more suitable for real-world applications.

Chapter 11: Industry-Specific Applications of LLM Agents

Large Language Model (LLM) agents are transforming industries by enabling new forms of automation, improving decision-making, and enhancing user interactions. From healthcare to finance, education, and customer service, LLM agents are increasingly being leveraged to improve outcomes and drive efficiency. This chapter will explore several key industries where LLM agents have made a significant impact, with a focus on practical applications and case studies. We will discuss the potential of LLM agents in healthcare, finance, education, and customer service, highlighting their roles in diagnostics, fraud detection, personalized learning, and customer support.

1. Healthcare

LLM agents are being used in healthcare to streamline processes, enhance decision-making, and improve patient outcomes. These agents can assist medical professionals by providing diagnostic assistance and offering real-time support to patients.

Diagnostic Assistance

LLM agents can assist healthcare professionals by providing diagnostic support, analyzing medical records, and suggesting potential diagnoses based on symptoms, test results, and patient history.

1. **Medical Data Analysis**:
    - o LLM agents can be trained on vast datasets of medical literature, clinical guidelines, and case studies to help doctors make informed decisions.
    - o By analyzing patient records, lab results, and historical data, these agents can suggest potential diagnoses or highlight conditions that require further investigation.
2. **Symptom Checking**:
    - o LLM agents can also be deployed in consumer-facing applications, allowing patients to input symptoms and receive potential causes, advice, or the recommendation to visit a healthcare professional.

- For example, an LLM agent could guide a patient to seek immediate medical attention if it detects symptoms of a serious condition like a heart attack or stroke.

Example: Diagnostic Assistance with GPT-3:

```
import openai

openai.api_key = "your-api-key-here"

def get_diagnosis(symptoms):
    prompt = f"Given the following symptoms: {symptoms}, what
are the potential diagnoses?"
    response = openai.Completion.create(
        engine="text-davinci-003",
        prompt=prompt,
        max_tokens=150
    )
    return response.choices[0].text.strip()

# Example usage
symptoms = "fever, cough, shortness of breath"
print(get_diagnosis(symptoms))
```

- This example demonstrates how an LLM agent could suggest possible diagnoses based on input symptoms.

Patient Interaction and Support

LLM agents can be deployed as virtual assistants to interact with patients, providing 24/7 support, answering medical queries, and managing appointments.

1. **Chatbots for Health Information**:
   - LLM agents can answer common questions about medications, treatments, and preventive measures, ensuring that patients receive accurate, consistent information.
   - These agents can be integrated into hospital websites or health apps, making it easier for patients to access information.
2. **Telemedicine Integration**:
   - LLM agents can support telemedicine platforms by assisting in preliminary consultations and collecting patient information before they speak with a doctor.

Example: Virtual Health Assistant for Appointment Scheduling:

```
class HealthAssistant:
    def __init__(self):
        self.appointments = {}

    def schedule_appointment(self, patient_name, date, time):
        self.appointments[patient_name] = f"Appointment
scheduled for {date} at {time}"
        return self.appointments[patient_name]

# Usage
assistant = HealthAssistant()
print(assistant.schedule_appointment("John Doe", "2025-03-
25", "10:00 AM"))
```

- This simplified example shows how an LLM agent could manage appointment scheduling by interacting with patients.

---

2. Finance

In the finance industry, LLM agents are being applied to improve decision-making, detect fraud, and automate trading. These applications help financial institutions increase efficiency and reduce risks.

Fraud Detection

LLM agents can analyze transaction data, identify unusual patterns, and flag potential fraudulent activities in real-time. By using historical data and machine learning models, these agents can detect anomalies that deviate from typical transaction patterns.

1. **Real-Time Monitoring**:
    o LLM agents can continuously monitor financial transactions across multiple accounts, detecting suspicious activities such as large or unusual transfers, multiple rapid transactions, or foreign transactions that don't match the user's typical behavior.
2. **Risk Assessment**:
    o By analyzing transaction history and external data sources (e.g., credit scores, geographic information), LLM agents can

provide real-time risk assessments, which can help prevent financial crimes like money laundering.

Example: Fraud Detection System:

```python
import random

class FraudDetection:
    def __init__(self):
        self.transaction_history = []

    def record_transaction(self, amount, country):
        self.transaction_history.append((amount, country))

    def detect_fraud(self, amount, country):
        # Simple rule-based fraud detection: flag
transactions over $10000 or from unfamiliar countries
        if amount > 10000 or country not in ["USA", "UK",
"Canada"]:
            return "Fraudulent transaction detected!"
        return "Transaction is safe."

# Usage
fraud_detector = FraudDetection()
fraud_detector.record_transaction(2000, "USA")
print(fraud_detector.detect_fraud(15000, "Germany"))
```

- In this example, a simple rule-based fraud detection system flags transactions that exceed a threshold or originate from unfamiliar countries.

Automated Trading Systems

LLM agents are also being used to automate trading by analyzing financial data and executing buy or sell orders based on predefined strategies.

1. **Algorithmic Trading**:
   o LLM agents can make decisions based on financial news, market trends, and technical indicators. By learning from historical market data, these agents can predict future price movements and execute trades accordingly.
2. **Sentiment Analysis**:
   o By analyzing news articles and social media posts, LLM agents can gauge market sentiment and make trading decisions based on public perception or specific events (e.g., company earnings reports or geopolitical events).

Example: Automated Trading System with Sentiment Analysis:

```python
import random

class TradingBot:
    def __init__(self):
        self.balance = 10000  # Initial balance in USD
        self.portfolio = {"stock_A": 0}

    def buy_stock(self, stock, amount, price):
        if self.balance >= amount * price:
            self.portfolio[stock] += amount
            self.balance -= amount * price
            return f"Bought {amount} of {stock} at {price}
each"
        return "Insufficient funds"

    def sell_stock(self, stock, amount, price):
        if self.portfolio[stock] >= amount:
            self.portfolio[stock] -= amount
            self.balance += amount * price
            return f"Sold {amount} of {stock} at {price}
each"
        return "Not enough stock to sell"

    def analyze_sentiment_and_trade(self, sentiment):
        if sentiment == "positive":
            return self.buy_stock("stock_A", 10,
random.uniform(50, 150))
        else:
            return self.sell_stock("stock_A", 10,
random.uniform(50, 150))

# Usage
bot = TradingBot()
print(bot.analyze_sentiment_and_trade("positive"))
```

- This example demonstrates how a simple automated trading system might buy or sell stocks based on market sentiment.

---

3. Education

LLM agents are revolutionizing education by providing personalized learning experiences, automating administrative tasks, and enhancing student engagement.

Personalized Learning Assistants

LLM agents can serve as personalized tutors that adapt to each student's learning style, pace, and preferences. These assistants can provide explanations, answer questions, and suggest study materials tailored to the individual's needs.

1. **Adaptive Learning**:
   - LLM agents can assess a student's strengths and weaknesses and adjust the difficulty of questions or learning materials accordingly.
2. **Interactive Q&A**:
   - Students can interact with LLM agents to get answers to their questions in real-time, enabling self-paced learning without needing constant human supervision.

Example: Personalized Learning Assistant:

```
class LearningAssistant:
    def __init__(self):
        self.student_progress = {}

    def track_progress(self, student_name, subject, score):
        if student_name not in self.student_progress:
            self.student_progress[student_name] = {}
        self.student_progress[student_name][subject] = score
        return f"Progress updated for {student_name} in
{subject}."

    def suggest_material(self, student_name):
        if student_name not in self.student_progress:
            return "No data available for this student."
        progress = self.student_progress[student_name]
        if "math" in progress and progress["math"] < 50:
            return "Suggested material: Advanced math problem
sets."
        return "Suggested material: General study guide."

# Usage
assistant = LearningAssistant()
print(assistant.track_progress("John Doe", "math", 45))
print(assistant.suggest_material("John Doe"))
```

- This example tracks a student's progress and recommends study materials based on performance.

Administrative Automation

LLM agents can also automate administrative tasks in educational institutions, such as scheduling classes, grading assignments, and managing student records.

1. **Classroom Management**:
   o LLM agents can assist teachers in scheduling classes, managing attendance, and even grading assignments based on predefined rubrics.
2. **Automated Feedback**:
   o LLM agents can generate automated feedback on assignments or exams, providing students with insights into areas where they can improve.

---

4. Customer Service

LLM agents are widely used in customer service to improve customer experience, streamline interactions, and provide real-time support.

Chatbots and Virtual Assistants

LLM-powered chatbots and virtual assistants can handle a wide range of customer queries, from simple FAQs to complex issues that require multi-turn conversations. These agents can operate 24/7, ensuring that customers always have access to support.

1. **Query Handling**:
   o Chatbots can respond to a wide array of customer queries, from product information to troubleshooting.
2. **Ticket Management**:
   o LLM agents can assist in managing support tickets, categorizing issues, and escalating more complex cases to human agents.

Example: Customer Service Chatbot:

```
class Chatbot:
    def __init__(self):
        self.responses = {
```

```
            "how do I reset my password": "Please visit the
'Forgot Password' page.",
            "what is your return policy": "You can return
items within 30 days of purchase."
        }

    def respond(self, query):
        query = query.lower()
        return self.responses.get(query, "Sorry, I didn't
understand that.")

# Usage
chatbot = Chatbot()
print(chatbot.respond("How do I reset my password?"))
```

- This example illustrates how a chatbot can respond to common customer queries.

Enhancing Customer Experience

LLM agents can enhance the overall customer experience by providing personalized interactions, analyzing customer sentiment, and offering relevant product recommendations.

1. **Sentiment Analysis**:
   o By analyzing the sentiment of customer interactions, LLM agents can tailor their responses, prioritizing more urgent or frustrated customers.
2. **Personalized Recommendations**:
   o Based on past purchases or preferences, LLM agents can recommend products or services that the customer is most likely to be interested in.

Example: Sentiment-Based Response Modification:

```
class SentimentBasedResponse:
    def __init__(self):
        self.responses = {
            "positive": "Thank you for your positive
feedback!",
            "neutral": "Thank you for your message. How can
we assist you?",
            "negative": "We're sorry to hear that. How can we
resolve the issue?"
        }
```

```
    def generate_response(self, sentiment):
        return self.responses.get(sentiment, "Sorry, I didn't
understand your sentiment.")

# Usage
response = SentimentBasedResponse()
print(response.generate_response("negative"))
```

- This example shows how a chatbot can modify its response based on the sentiment of the customer.

LLM agents are playing an increasingly important role across various industries by enhancing efficiency, improving decision-making, and providing personalized, real-time interactions. In healthcare, they assist with diagnostics and patient support; in finance, they are used for fraud detection and trading; in education, they provide personalized learning experiences; and in customer service, they improve customer engagement through chatbots and virtual assistants. By harnessing the power of LLM agents, industries can achieve greater automation, streamline operations, and enhance the overall experience for customers, patients, and clients.

Chapter 12: Innovative and Emerging Use Cases

As Large Language Model (LLM) technology continues to advance, its applications extend beyond traditional use cases like customer service and healthcare. In this chapter, we will explore some of the most innovative and emerging use cases where LLM agents are having a transformative impact. These use cases span a wide range of industries, from creative sectors like content generation and gaming to smart homes, robotics, and legal compliance. By leveraging the capabilities of LLM agents, these industries can achieve greater efficiency, creativity, and automation.

1. Creative Industries

LLM agents are revolutionizing the creative industries by enhancing content creation, supporting creative decision-making, and providing new forms of interactive entertainment.

Content Generation and Curation

1. **Content Generation**:
    - LLM agents are being used to generate high-quality written content at scale. From blog posts to news articles, product descriptions, and social media content, LLMs can assist in producing a wide range of written materials.
    - These agents can be trained on specific datasets related to a brand or industry, ensuring the generated content aligns with the required tone, style, and subject matter.
2. **Content Curation**:
    - Content curation involves selecting and organizing content for specific audiences. LLM agents can automatically gather relevant articles, videos, and other media based on specific topics or user interests.
    - By analyzing user behavior, preferences, and trends, these agents can personalize the content suggestions to improve engagement.

Example: Content Generation with GPT-3:

```
import openai
```

```
openai.api_key = "your-api-key-here"

def generate_content(topic):
    prompt = f"Write an informative blog post about {topic}."
    response = openai.Completion.create(
        engine="text-davinci-003",
        prompt=prompt,
        max_tokens=500
    )
    return response.choices[0].text.strip()

# Example usage
topic = "The Future of AI in Healthcare"
print(generate_content(topic))
```

- This example uses GPT-3 to generate a blog post based on a given topic, which could be used for content marketing or educational purposes.

Interactive Storytelling and Gaming

1. **Interactive Storytelling**:
   o LLM agents can create immersive, interactive narratives in real-time. By processing user inputs, these agents can adapt the story, introduce new plot twists, and develop characters dynamically.
   o Games and interactive fiction are increasingly using LLM agents to allow players to engage in complex conversations with characters, influencing the story's direction based on choices made by the player.
2. **Gaming NPCs (Non-Player Characters)**:
   o Traditional NPCs follow predefined scripts, but with LLM agents, NPCs can engage in dynamic, context-aware conversations with players, making the gaming experience feel more interactive and personalized.

Example: Interactive Storytelling with GPT-3:

```
import openai

openai.api_key = "your-api-key-here"

def interactive_story(input_text):
    prompt = f"Create an interactive story based on this
input: {input_text}. Respond with a choice for the player."
```

```
    response = openai.Completion.create(
        engine="text-davinci-003",
        prompt=prompt,
        max_tokens=150
    )
    return response.choices[0].text.strip()

# Example usage
input_text = "You enter a dark forest and see two paths ahead
of you."
print(interactive_story(input_text))
```

- This example generates an interactive story based on the player's input, allowing them to make choices that influence the narrative.

---

2. Smart Homes and IoT

The integration of LLM agents with smart home technologies and the Internet of Things (IoT) is enabling greater automation, convenience, and personalization in our living spaces.

Home Automation and Control

1. **Voice Assistants**:
   - LLM agents are commonly used in voice-activated smart home assistants (e.g., Amazon Alexa, Google Assistant) to control various devices in the home, such as lights, thermostats, and security systems.
   - By understanding natural language commands, LLM agents make it easier for users to interact with their smart homes without needing specialized knowledge or technical skills.
2. **Automated Task Management**:
   - LLM agents can automate everyday tasks in the home, such as adjusting the temperature, managing grocery lists, or setting reminders. These agents can also learn user preferences and optimize settings based on past behavior.

Example: Home Automation with Voice Commands:

```
import pyttsx3
import speech_recognition as sr
```

```
# Initialize speech engine
engine = pyttsx3.init()

def listen_for_commands():
    recognizer = sr.Recognizer()
    with sr.Microphone() as source:
        print("Listening for commands...")
        audio = recognizer.listen(source)

    try:
        command = recognizer.recognize_google(audio)
        print(f"Command received: {command}")
        return command.lower()
    except sr.UnknownValueError:
        return "Sorry, I didn't understand that."

def execute_command(command):
    if "turn on the lights" in command:
        print("Turning on the lights.")
        engine.say("Turning on the lights")
        engine.runAndWait()
    elif "set temperature to" in command:
        temp = command.split()[-1]
        print(f"Setting temperature to {temp} degrees.")
        engine.say(f"Setting temperature to {temp} degrees.")
        engine.runAndWait()

# Listen for command and execute
command = listen_for_commands()
execute_command(command)
```

- This example uses speech recognition to process voice commands and control smart devices, such as turning on lights or adjusting the temperature.

Integration with Smart Devices

1. **Smart Appliances**:
   o LLM agents can also integrate with IoT-enabled appliances (e.g., smart fridges, washing machines) to provide users with real-time status updates, reminders, and troubleshooting advice.
2. **Personalized Environment Settings**:
   o By integrating with IoT devices, LLM agents can personalize the home environment based on user preferences. For example, an agent might automatically adjust the lighting,

temperature, and media playback based on the time of day or the user's mood.

---

3. Robotics

Robotics is one of the most exciting areas where LLM agents are making significant strides, particularly in areas like autonomous navigation and human-robot interaction.

Autonomous Navigation and Control

1. **Navigation in Dynamic Environments**:
   - o LLM agents enable robots to understand and navigate complex environments autonomously. They can interpret sensor data, plan paths, avoid obstacles, and adapt to new situations without human intervention.
   - o Whether it's a robot navigating a warehouse or a delivery robot moving through crowded streets, LLM agents can make real-time decisions about the best path to take.
2. **Simultaneous Localization and Mapping (SLAM)**:
   - o SLAM algorithms allow robots to build a map of their environment while simultaneously determining their position within it. LLM agents can integrate with SLAM to enable robots to navigate without relying on preexisting maps.

Example: Path Planning for Autonomous Robots:

```python
import numpy as np

class RobotNavigator:
    def __init__(self, grid_size):
        self.grid_size = grid_size
        self.position = (0, 0)

    def move(self, direction):
        x, y = self.position
        if direction == "up" and x > 0:
            self.position = (x - 1, y)
        elif direction == "down" and x < self.grid_size - 1:
            self.position = (x + 1, y)
        elif direction == "left" and y > 0:
            self.position = (x, y - 1)
```

```
        elif direction == "right" and y < self.grid_size - 1:
            self.position = (x, y + 1)
        return self.position

# Usage
robot = RobotNavigator(5)
print(robot.move("up"))
print(robot.move("right"))
```

- This simple example demonstrates path planning by moving the robot in a grid. In real-world applications, robots would navigate using more complex algorithms, such as A* or Dijkstra's algorithm.

Human-Robot Interaction

1. **Natural Language Communication**:
   - LLM agents enhance human-robot interaction by enabling robots to understand and respond to natural language commands. This can include voice commands or text-based interactions.
   - By using LLM agents, robots can engage in more sophisticated dialogues with humans, improving the user experience.
2. **Social Robotics**:
   - Social robots, designed to interact with humans in more natural ways, can use LLM agents to interpret emotions, respond empathetically, and adapt their behavior based on human interaction.

Example: Human-Robot Conversation:

```
class SocialRobot:
    def __init__(self):
        self.name = "RoboFriend"

    def greet(self, user_name):
        return f"Hello, {user_name}! How can I assist you
today?"

    def respond(self, command):
        responses = {
            "help": "I am here to assist you with tasks.",
            "shutdown": "Shutting down. See you later!"
        }
        return responses.get(command.lower(), "I'm sorry, I
didn't understand that.")
```

```
# Usage
robot = SocialRobot()
print(robot.greet("Alice"))
print(robot.respond("help"))
```

- This example shows how a social robot can interact with a human by understanding simple commands and responding accordingly.

---

4. Legal and Compliance

In the legal and compliance industries, LLM agents are playing a crucial role in streamlining processes, reducing the risk of errors, and automating tedious tasks such as document analysis and compliance monitoring.

Document Analysis and Management

1. **Contract Review**:
   - LLM agents can be used to review contracts and legal documents, identifying key clauses, terms, and potential risks. These agents can flag unusual or non-standard clauses, helping lawyers quickly spot critical issues.
   - LLM agents can also extract information from large volumes of legal documents, organizing it for easier analysis.
2. **Compliance Document Automation**:
   - LLM agents can automate the process of drafting compliance documents, ensuring that all necessary regulations and legal requirements are met.

Example: Document Analysis for Contract Review:

```
import openai

openai.api_key = "your-api-key-here"

def analyze_contract(contract_text):
    prompt = f"Analyze the following contract and identify
any risks or unusual clauses: {contract_text}"
    response = openai.Completion.create(
        engine="text-davinci-003",
        prompt=prompt,
        max_tokens=300
    )
```

```
    return response.choices[0].text.strip()
```

```
# Example usage
contract = "This contract shall remain valid for 2 years from
the date of signing, and both parties must give 30 days'
notice for termination."
print(analyze_contract(contract))
```

- This example uses GPT-3 to analyze a contract and identify potential risks or unusual clauses.

Automated Compliance Monitoring

1. **Regulatory Monitoring**:
   - o LLM agents can monitor and interpret changes in regulatory frameworks, ensuring that organizations stay compliant with local, national, and international laws.
   - o By analyzing legal texts, regulatory updates, and compliance documents, LLM agents can flag areas where the organization might be at risk.

Example: Compliance Monitoring with GPT-3:

```
def monitor_compliance(change_description):
    prompt = f"Based on the following regulatory change:
{change_description}, what actions should the company take to
remain compliant?"
    response = openai.Completion.create(
        engine="text-davinci-003",
        prompt=prompt,
        max_tokens=250
    )
    return response.choices[0].text.strip()
```

```
# Example usage
regulatory_change = "New data privacy laws require companies
to provide users with more control over their personal data."
print(monitor_compliance(regulatory_change))
```

- This example demonstrates how an LLM agent can analyze regulatory changes and provide actionable advice for compliance.

LLM agents are increasingly being applied to innovative and emerging use cases across a variety of industries. From transforming content creation in the creative industries to enhancing home automation in smart homes, autonomous navigation in robotics, and improving compliance in the legal sector, the potential applications of LLM agents are vast. As these agents continue to evolve, they will further drive automation, creativity, and efficiency, reshaping how businesses and individuals interact with technology.

Chapter 13: Real-World Success Stories

The impact of Large Language Model (LLM) agents is becoming increasingly apparent across various industries. Real-world case studies not only demonstrate the practical application of these technologies but also provide valuable insights into the challenges, successes, and lessons learned during their implementation. In this chapter, we will explore several case studies from industries like healthcare, finance, education, and customer service, highlighting the tangible benefits and challenges of integrating LLM agents into real-world operations.

1. Case Study 1: AI in Healthcare Diagnostics

Problem Statement

The healthcare industry faces the challenge of accurately diagnosing a wide range of medical conditions, especially with limited access to specialists in remote or underserved areas. Timely and accurate diagnoses are critical to improving patient outcomes, but human limitations in terms of knowledge, availability, and capacity can lead to delays or errors.

Healthcare professionals must sift through vast amounts of medical data, patient histories, lab reports, and medical research to make informed decisions. This is where LLM agents, with their ability to process large datasets and synthesize knowledge, can play a transformative role in assisting medical professionals in diagnostics.

Implementation Details

A healthcare organization partnered with a technology provider to deploy an AI-powered diagnostic assistant that utilized an LLM agent. The system was trained on a comprehensive dataset of medical records, research papers, and diagnostic guidelines, and integrated with electronic health record (EHR) systems to analyze patient data in real-time.

The key components of the implementation included:

1. **Data Integration**: The LLM agent was integrated with EHR systems to access and analyze patient data, such as symptoms, medical history, test results, and previous diagnoses.
2. **Natural Language Processing (NLP)**: The LLM agent used advanced NLP techniques to interpret free-text medical notes, allowing it to extract relevant information from physician notes and historical medical documents.
3. **Diagnostic Recommendations**: The LLM agent provided diagnostic suggestions based on symptoms, test results, and medical history, offering doctors a second opinion and assisting them in prioritizing the most likely diagnoses.

Outcomes and Lessons Learned

Outcomes:

- **Improved Diagnostic Accuracy**: The AI-powered diagnostic assistant increased diagnostic accuracy by flagging conditions that might have been overlooked by healthcare professionals.
- **Efficiency Gains**: Physicians were able to process patient information more quickly, reducing the time it took to make a diagnosis and improving workflow efficiency.
- **Reduction in Errors**: The LLM agent helped reduce human error by cross-referencing patient data with up-to-date medical literature, providing a more holistic view of the patient's condition.

Lessons Learned:

- **Data Quality**: Ensuring that the data used to train the LLM agent was clean, comprehensive, and accurate was critical to the system's effectiveness.
- **Human Oversight**: While the AI provided valuable recommendations, human oversight was necessary to verify diagnoses and ensure that patient safety was never compromised.
- **Integration Challenges**: Integrating the AI system with existing healthcare systems required careful planning, particularly in terms of ensuring seamless data exchange and maintaining privacy compliance (e.g., HIPAA).

2. Case Study 2: Financial Fraud Detection Using LLM Agents

Challenges and Solutions

Financial institutions deal with the constant threat of fraud, whether through identity theft, account hacking, or phishing attacks. Detecting fraudulent activities in real-time is crucial to minimize losses and protect customers. Traditional fraud detection systems, while effective, often rely on rule-based algorithms that can be circumvented by more sophisticated fraudulent schemes.

Challenges:

1. **Evolving Fraud Techniques**: Fraudulent activities are constantly evolving, requiring fraud detection systems to adapt quickly.
2. **Data Volume**: Financial institutions process millions of transactions every day, making it difficult to detect fraud in real-time without highly advanced systems.

Solution: An LLM-powered fraud detection system was deployed to analyze transaction patterns and identify potentially fraudulent activities by using advanced machine learning techniques. The system utilized historical transaction data, user behavior patterns, and external data sources (e.g., blacklists, credit reports) to provide a more robust fraud detection system.

Technical Implementation

1. **Data Collection**: The system integrated with the bank's transactional database, as well as external data sources like credit bureaus, to track real-time transactions and customer profiles.
2. **Model Training**: The LLM agent was trained on historical transaction data, using supervised learning techniques to learn patterns associated with legitimate and fraudulent transactions.
3. **Real-Time Monitoring**: The system used anomaly detection algorithms to flag transactions that deviated from normal user behavior, such as unusual spending patterns or transactions from foreign locations.
4. **Adaptive Learning**: The system was designed to adapt to new fraud patterns by continuously retraining the model with updated transaction data.

Impact on Operations

1. **Real-Time Detection**: The LLM agent enabled real-time fraud detection, reducing the response time and enabling the bank to immediately halt fraudulent transactions.
2. **Reduced False Positives**: By using a more sophisticated model, the system reduced the number of legitimate transactions falsely flagged as fraud, improving customer satisfaction.
3. **Scalability**: The AI system was able to handle large volumes of transactions with minimal computational overhead, allowing the bank to scale its fraud detection efforts across a global customer base.

---

3. Case Study 3: Educational Personalized Learning Assistant

Design and Development

An educational institution sought to implement an LLM-powered personalized learning assistant for its online courses. The goal was to provide students with an AI-powered assistant that could help them learn at their own pace, answering questions, providing explanations, and offering feedback on assignments.

Design Considerations:

1. **Student Data Integration**: The assistant needed access to student performance data, including grades, assignment submissions, and activity logs, to tailor its interactions.
2. **Natural Language Processing**: The assistant used NLP to understand student queries, provide contextual answers, and explain complex concepts in a way that matched the student's level of understanding.

User Feedback and Effectiveness

1. **Personalized Learning Paths**: Based on each student's performance, the assistant recommended customized study materials and exercises. For instance, if a student struggled with a particular math concept, the assistant would recommend additional resources and practice problems.

2. **Instant Feedback**: The assistant was able to provide real-time feedback on assignments, offering suggestions for improvement and explaining mistakes.
3. **24/7 Availability**: Students could interact with the assistant at any time, providing flexibility and ensuring that support was available whenever needed.

User Feedback:

- **Positive Engagement**: Students reported higher engagement with their learning materials, as they appreciated the immediate feedback and personalized recommendations.
- **Improved Performance**: Many students showed improvement in test scores, attributed to the tailored assistance they received.

Future Enhancements

1. **Adaptive Learning Algorithms**: Future updates would incorporate more sophisticated adaptive learning algorithms that could better predict student difficulties and provide even more personalized learning experiences.
2. **Integration with Other Learning Tools**: The next phase involved integrating the assistant with video lectures and other multimedia resources to make the learning experience more interactive.

---

4. Case Study 4: Customer Service Chatbot Deployment

Deployment Strategy

A major retailer decided to deploy an LLM-powered chatbot to handle customer service inquiries on its website and mobile app. The chatbot's primary tasks included answering product-related questions, assisting with order tracking, handling returns, and resolving general customer issues.

Deployment Approach:

1. **Platform Integration**: The chatbot was integrated with the retailer's existing customer service platforms, including their CRM and order management systems, to provide personalized and accurate responses.

2. **Multilingual Support**: The chatbot was designed to handle inquiries in multiple languages, enabling the retailer to provide global customer support.
3. **Training and Customization**: The chatbot was trained on the retailer's customer service transcripts, FAQs, and product information to ensure that it provided relevant and accurate responses.

Performance Metrics

The success of the chatbot was evaluated using several key performance indicators (KPIs):

1. **Response Time**: The chatbot successfully reduced the average response time for customer inquiries from several minutes to just a few seconds.
2. **Resolution Rate**: The chatbot was able to resolve approximately 80% of customer inquiries without needing to escalate to a human agent.
3. **Customer Satisfaction**: Post-interaction surveys revealed that 85% of users were satisfied with the chatbot's responses, indicating a high level of effectiveness.

Example of Chatbot Performance Metrics:

```
# Metrics tracking
responses_handled = 1200
successful_resolutions = 960
customer_satisfaction = 85  # Percentage

def calculate_resolution_rate(successful_resolutions,
responses_handled):
    return (successful_resolutions / responses_handled) * 100

def calculate_satisfaction_rate(customer_satisfaction,
responses_handled):
    return (customer_satisfaction * responses_handled) / 100

resolution_rate =
calculate_resolution_rate(successful_resolutions,
responses_handled)
satisfaction_rate =
calculate_satisfaction_rate(customer_satisfaction,
responses_handled)

print(f"Resolution Rate: {resolution_rate}%")
```

```
print(f"Satisfaction Rate: {satisfaction_rate} out of
{responses_handled}")
```

- This code calculates the resolution rate and satisfaction rate based on the chatbot's performance data, providing insights into its overall effectiveness.

Customer Satisfaction Results

The chatbot deployment led to increased customer satisfaction for several reasons:

1. **24/7 Support**: Customers could receive assistance at any time, which was particularly beneficial for those in different time zones.
2. **Reduced Wait Times**: Customers no longer had to wait in long queues to speak with human agents, improving their overall experience.
3. **Consistency**: The chatbot provided consistent answers to frequently asked questions, reducing the potential for human error.

These case studies demonstrate the diverse and impactful ways in which LLM agents are being applied across various industries. In healthcare, LLMs assist with diagnostics and patient support;

in finance, they help detect fraud and automate trading; in education, they enhance personalized learning experiences; and in customer service, they improve response times and customer satisfaction. By examining these real-world examples, we gain valuable insights into the challenges, solutions, and potential for further improvements in LLM agent deployment. The lessons learned from these case studies can guide future implementations and ensure that LLM agents continue to drive innovation across industries.

Chapter 14: Ethical Considerations in LLM Agent Development

As Large Language Models (LLMs) continue to evolve and become integrated into more aspects of society, ethical considerations have become increasingly important. Developing and deploying LLM agents responsibly involves addressing issues related to bias, fairness, privacy, transparency, and sustainability. In this chapter, we will explore the key ethical concerns in LLM agent development and provide strategies for mitigating potential risks. These concerns are crucial not only for building trustworthy and effective systems but also for ensuring that LLM agents contribute positively to society.

1. Bias and Fairness

Identifying and Mitigating Bias in LLMs

Bias in machine learning models, including LLM agents, refers to the systematic and unfair discrimination against certain groups or outcomes due to the data used for training. Because LLMs are often trained on vast amounts of publicly available data, they may inherit biases present in that data, such as racial, gender, or socio-economic biases.

Types of Bias:

1. **Data Bias**: If the training data is not representative of diverse perspectives or is skewed in favor of certain groups, the LLM agent may exhibit biased behavior.
2. **Algorithmic Bias**: Even with diverse data, the algorithms used to train LLMs may amplify or introduce bias, leading to unfair decision-making.

Mitigation Strategies:

1. **Bias Audits**: Regularly auditing models for bias using fairness metrics can help identify areas where the model may be producing biased outputs.
2. **Diverse Training Data**: Ensuring that training data represents diverse populations, contexts, and scenarios is crucial for reducing bias.

3. **Fairness Constraints**: Implementing fairness constraints during the model training process can help ensure that the model's predictions do not disproportionately disadvantage any particular group.

Example: Bias Detection and Mitigation in LLMs

```python
from sklearn.metrics import confusion_matrix
import numpy as np

# Simulated predicted vs true values (e.g., gender bias
detection)
predictions = ['male', 'female', 'female', 'male', 'male',
'female']
true_labels = ['female', 'female', 'female', 'male', 'male',
'male']

# Confusion matrix to check bias in predictions
cm = confusion_matrix(true_labels, predictions,
labels=['male', 'female'])
print("Confusion Matrix:")
print(cm)

# Calculate fairness metrics (e.g., equal opportunity or
accuracy disparity)
accuracy_male = cm[0, 0] / (cm[0, 0] + cm[0, 1])
accuracy_female = cm[1, 1] / (cm[1, 0] + cm[1, 1])

print(f"Accuracy for Male: {accuracy_male}")
print(f"Accuracy for Female: {accuracy_female}")
```

In this example, a confusion matrix is used to check if predictions are equally accurate across different groups (e.g., male vs female). This method helps to identify bias in classification tasks and ensure fairness.

Ensuring Fairness in Decision-Making

1. **Fairness Definitions**: There are multiple definitions of fairness, such as:
   - **Equality of Opportunity**: Ensuring that every group has equal chances of success.
   - **Individual Fairness**: Ensuring that similar individuals are treated similarly.

2. **Fairness Metrics**: Fairness metrics like demographic parity, equalized odds, and disparate impact can help assess whether the model is behaving fairly.

Example: Implementing Fairness Constraints in Model Training

```python
from fairness import DemographicParity
from sklearn.metrics import accuracy_score

# Assume X_train, y_train are the training data and labels
# Fit a model (e.g., logistic regression)
model = LogisticRegression()
model.fit(X_train, y_train)

# Evaluate fairness using Demographic Parity
dp = DemographicParity()
fairness_score = dp.evaluate(model, X_train, y_train)

print(f"Fairness score: {fairness_score}")
```

In this example, we use fairness metrics like **Demographic Parity** to assess if a model's predictions are fair across different groups.

---

2. Privacy and Data Protection

GDPR and Other Regulatory Frameworks

As LLM agents are deployed in various sectors, particularly in areas like healthcare, finance, and customer service, privacy and data protection become paramount. Regulations like the **General Data Protection Regulation (GDPR)** in the European Union impose strict requirements on how personal data is collected, processed, and stored.

Key Aspects of GDPR:

1. **Data Minimization**: Only collect the data necessary for the specific task at hand.
2. **Right to Access and Portability**: Users have the right to access and transfer their data across systems.

3. **Right to Erasure (Right to be Forgotten)**: Users can request that their data be deleted from a system.
4. **Transparency and Consent**: Users should be informed about how their data will be used and should provide explicit consent.

Best Practices for Data Privacy

1. **Data Anonymization**:
   o Sensitive data can be anonymized to reduce privacy risks. Techniques like **k-anonymity**, **differential privacy**, and **data masking** can ensure that individuals' identities are protected while still allowing the data to be useful.
2. **Encryption**:
   o Ensuring that data is encrypted both in transit and at rest protects it from unauthorized access or theft.
3. **Access Control**:
   o Limiting access to sensitive data to authorized personnel only helps protect privacy.

Example: Data Anonymization

python

```python
import pandas as pd
from sklearn.preprocessing import LabelEncoder

# Sample data with sensitive information
data = pd.DataFrame({
    'name': ['Alice', 'Bob', 'Charlie', 'David'],
    'email': ['alice@example.com', 'bob@example.com',
'charlie@example.com', 'david@example.com'],
    'age': [25, 30, 35, 40]
})

# Anonymize the 'name' column
label_encoder = LabelEncoder()
data['name'] = label_encoder.fit_transform(data['name'])

print("Anonymized Data:")
print(data)
```

In this example, sensitive information (such as names) is anonymized using a label encoding technique, which converts names into unique numerical identifiers.

3. Accountability and Transparency

Explainable AI (XAI)

Explainable AI (XAI) refers to the practice of developing AI models that are interpretable and understandable to humans. It is especially important in fields like healthcare, finance, and law, where decisions made by AI systems can have significant consequences.

1. **Why XAI is Important**:
    - **Trust**: Stakeholders (users, patients, customers) need to trust AI systems. If they can understand why a decision was made, they are more likely to trust the system.
    - **Accountability**: When decisions made by AI agents need to be justified (e.g., in a court of law), XAI allows for transparency and accountability.

Transparent Decision-Making Processes

1. **Model Transparency**: Ensuring that the decision-making process is not a "black box" is vital for ethical AI development. This can be achieved by using interpretable models like decision trees, or by applying techniques like LIME or SHAP to explain the behavior of complex models like deep neural networks.

Example: Explainable Model with LIME

```python
import lime
from lime.lime_tabular import LimeTabularExplainer
import numpy as np
from sklearn.datasets import load_iris
from sklearn.ensemble import RandomForestClassifier

# Load the iris dataset
data = load_iris()
X, y = data.data, data.target

# Train a random forest classifier
model = RandomForestClassifier()
model.fit(X, y)
```

```
# Explain a prediction using LIME
explainer = LimeTabularExplainer(X, training_labels=y,
mode="classification")
explanation = explainer.explain_instance(X[0],
model.predict_proba)

# Display the explanation
explanation.show_in_notebook()
```

- This example uses **LIME (Local Interpretable Model-agnostic Explanations)** to provide a local explanation for a prediction made by a RandomForest classifier, helping users understand the factors influencing the model's decision.

---

4. Sustainability and Environmental Impact

Energy Consumption of LLMs

Training and running LLMs can be computationally expensive, leading to high energy consumption and environmental impact. The large-scale hardware required to train state-of-the-art models like GPT-3 consumes a significant amount of electricity, contributing to carbon emissions.

1. **Carbon Footprint**: The training of large models can result in a substantial carbon footprint, which is a concern for sustainability in AI research and development.
2. **Efficiency Considerations**: Developing models that are smaller yet equally effective can help reduce the environmental impact.

Strategies for Sustainable AI Development

1. **Model Efficiency**:
   o Using techniques like **model distillation** and **quantization** can reduce the size and complexity of models, thereby lowering their energy consumption.
2. **Energy-Efficient Hardware**:
   o Using energy-efficient hardware such as specialized AI chips (e.g., **Google TPUs, NVIDIA GPUs**) can significantly reduce the energy required for both training and inference.
3. **Green AI**:

- o Researchers are increasingly focusing on "Green AI," which emphasizes improving the environmental efficiency of AI models without sacrificing performance.

Example: Energy-Efficient Model Distillation

python

```python
import torch
import torch.nn as nn
import torch.optim as optim

# Define a simple neural network (student model)
class SmallModel(nn.Module):
    def __init__(self):
        super(SmallModel, self).__init__()
        self.fc = nn.Linear(10, 2)

    def forward(self, x):
        return self.fc(x)

# Define a larger, pre-trained model (teacher model)
class LargeModel(nn.Module):
    def __init__(self):
        super(LargeModel, self).__init__()
        self.fc = nn.Linear(10, 2)

    def forward(self, x):
        return self.fc(x)

# Training setup (distillation process)
teacher = LargeModel()
student = SmallModel()

# Use teacher's soft targets to train the student model
loss_fn = nn.MSELoss()
optimizer = optim.SGD(student.parameters(), lr=0.01)

# Example distillation process
input_data = torch.randn(10, 10)
teacher_output = teacher(input_data)
student_output = student(input_data)
loss = loss_fn(student_output, teacher_output)

# Backpropagation
optimizer.zero_grad()
loss.backward()
optimizer.step()

print("Student model trained with distillation.")
```

- This code demonstrates a simplified **distillation** process, where a smaller model (student) learns from the outputs (soft targets) of a larger, pre-trained model (teacher), reducing computational and energy costs.

Ethical considerations are fundamental to the responsible development and deployment of LLM agents. Addressing concerns such as bias, fairness, privacy, transparency, and sustainability ensures that AI systems contribute positively to society and minimize harm. By implementing practices such as bias audits, adhering to privacy regulations like GDPR, ensuring explainable decision-making, and adopting sustainable AI practices, developers can create LLM agents that are not only effective but also ethical and responsible. As LLM technology continues to evolve, these considerations will remain central to its development and integration into real-world applications.

Chapter 15: Legal and Regulatory Compliance

As AI technologies, particularly Large Language Models (LLMs), become increasingly integrated into various industries, it is essential to consider the legal and regulatory frameworks that govern their development and use. Navigating these legal complexities ensures that LLM agents are deployed responsibly, ethically, and in compliance with local and international regulations. This chapter delves into the key legal and regulatory considerations surrounding AI, including navigating global laws, intellectual property, liability, and the implementation of ethical AI frameworks. We will explore how developers can ensure compliance while managing risks effectively.

1. Navigating AI Regulations

Overview of Global AI Laws and Standards

AI regulation is still an evolving area of law, with countries and regions taking different approaches to governing the development and use of AI technologies. While there is no single, unified set of global standards for AI, several regulatory frameworks and guidelines have been established to address ethical, safety, and privacy concerns.

Key Global AI Regulations:

1. **General Data Protection Regulation (GDPR)**: In the European Union, the GDPR has set strict guidelines regarding data privacy and protection. The regulation requires organizations to obtain explicit consent from individuals before collecting their data and gives individuals the right to request access to, rectification, or erasure of their personal data.
   - **Article 22**: This section of GDPR specifically addresses the use of automated decision-making, including profiling, and provides individuals with the right to contest decisions made solely by automated systems.
2. **AI Act (EU)**: The European Union's proposed **Artificial Intelligence Act** seeks to regulate AI technologies according to their risk levels. High-risk applications, such as AI in healthcare or finance, will

require more stringent oversight, including transparency, accountability, and human oversight.

- o **Risk Classification**: The EU AI Act categorizes AI systems based on their potential risks, ranging from minimal risk (e.g., AI chatbots) to high risk (e.g., AI used in critical infrastructure).

3. **AI Ethics Guidelines (OECD)**: The Organization for Economic Co-operation and Development (OECD) has established guidelines to promote AI development that is ethical, transparent, and accountable. These guidelines encourage the responsible development of AI by governments, developers, and organizations.

4. **China's AI Regulations**: China has begun implementing regulations aimed at controlling AI development to ensure its alignment with national interests. These regulations focus on AI's ethical use, privacy protection, and addressing potential biases.

Compliance Strategies for Developers: To navigate these complex regulations, developers should:

1. **Stay Informed**: Keeping up with global AI laws is critical. Regulations are evolving rapidly, and it's essential to stay informed about new laws that may affect AI deployments.

2. **Data Privacy Compliance**: Ensure AI systems comply with data protection laws, such as GDPR, by implementing privacy-by-design principles. This includes anonymizing sensitive data and securing users' consent.

Risk Management: Classify AI systems based on their risk levels (as per frameworks like the EU AI Act) and apply appropriate compliance measures, including transparency, safety testing, and human oversight.

Example: GDPR Compliance for AI Systems

python

```
# Simulating data anonymization for GDPR compliance
import pandas as pd

# Sample data
data = pd.DataFrame({
    'name': ['Alice', 'Bob', 'Charlie'],
    'email': ['alice@example.com', 'bob@example.com',
'charlie@example.com'],
    'age': [25, 30, 35]
```

```
})

# Anonymize the data (e.g., replacing names with unique
identifiers)
data['name'] = data['name'].apply(lambda x: hash(x))

print(data)
```

- In this example, personal data such as names and emails are
  anonymized to ensure privacy, which is crucial for GDPR
  compliance.

---

2. Intellectual Property Considerations

Protecting AI Innovations

Intellectual property (IP) laws are essential for protecting the innovations
developed in the AI space. As LLMs and other AI technologies become
more advanced, it is crucial to understand how intellectual property applies
to these developments.

Types of Intellectual Property for AI:

1. **Patents**: AI systems and algorithms that involve novel and non-
   obvious techniques can be patented. For example, an innovative
   algorithm used in an LLM might be patented to prevent others from
   using it without permission.
   - **Challenges with AI Patents**: One challenge is determining
     whether an AI system or model can be considered an
     "inventor" for patent purposes, as current patent laws may not
     fully recognize the role of AI in invention.
2. **Copyright**: The outputs of AI systems, such as generated text,
   images, or music, may be subject to copyright protection. However,
   the question arises: who owns the copyright—the developer, the
   organization, or the AI itself? In most cases, copyright is granted to
   the creator (i.e., the developer or organization).
   - **Fair Use**: Developers should be cautious about using large
     datasets to train LLMs, ensuring that they are not violating
     copyright laws or using copyrighted content without
     permission.

3. **Trade Secrets**: The underlying code, algorithms, and architectures used in AI systems may be considered trade secrets, providing protection without needing to disclose the details publicly.

Licensing and Usage Rights

1. **Open-Source Licensing**: Many LLM models are released under open-source licenses (e.g., MIT, Apache), which specify the conditions under which the model can be used, modified, or redistributed. Developers should ensure that they comply with these licenses when using or distributing open-source AI models.
2. **Commercial Licensing**: For proprietary LLM technologies, organizations may require commercial licenses to use, distribute, or modify the software. Negotiating clear licensing agreements is crucial to protect both the developers' and users' rights.

Example: Licensing and Usage Rights

python

```
# License agreement check for using an AI model
def check_license(model_name, license_type):
    if license_type == "Open Source":
        print(f"Using {model_name} under an open-source
license.")
    elif license_type == "Commercial":
        print(f"Ensure compliance with commercial license
terms for {model_name}.")
    else:
        print("Unknown license type.")

check_license("GPT-3", "Commercial")
```

- This function ensures that the developer is aware of the licensing conditions when using an AI model, ensuring compliance with either open-source or commercial terms.

---

3. Liability and Accountability

Legal Responsibility for AI Actions

As AI systems, including LLM agents, are deployed in critical applications (e.g., healthcare, finance, autonomous vehicles), the issue of liability for AI decisions becomes increasingly important. Determining who is responsible when an AI system causes harm or fails to perform its intended function is complex.

1. **AI as an Autonomous Actor**: Traditional legal frameworks were designed with human actors in mind, but AI systems, especially those that make autonomous decisions, challenge the allocation of responsibility. If an LLM agent provides incorrect medical advice that harms a patient, who is liable—the developer, the healthcare provider, or the AI itself?
2. **Product Liability**: In many cases, the liability for AI systems falls on the manufacturer or developer. For example, if an AI system malfunctions, causing harm to users or property, the developer may be held accountable under product liability laws.

Risk Management in AI Deployments

1. **Risk Assessment**: Developers should conduct a thorough risk assessment of AI deployments to identify potential legal, ethical, and operational risks. This includes assessing the likelihood of failures, harms, or unethical behavior from the AI system.
2. **Insurance**: Some organizations may opt for insurance to cover the potential risks of deploying AI systems, especially in high-risk sectors like healthcare or finance.

Example: Liability Assessment in AI Systems

python

```python
class AILiability:
    def __init__(self, ai_system, failure_risk):
        self.ai_system = ai_system
        self.failure_risk = failure_risk

    def assess_liability(self):
        if self.failure_risk > 0.5:
            return f"The liability risk for {self.ai_system} is high. Consider insurance or mitigation strategies."
        return f"The liability risk for {self.ai_system} is manageable."

# Usage
ai_system = AILiability("Medical Diagnostic AI", 0.7)
```

```
print(ai_system.assess_liability())
```

- This simple example assesses the risk of liability based on the failure risk of the AI system, guiding developers to make informed decisions about risk mitigation.

---

4. Ethical AI Frameworks

Implementing Ethical Guidelines in Development

Ethical AI frameworks provide guidance for creating AI systems that align with societal values and prevent harm. These frameworks are essential for ensuring that AI technologies are developed and used in a way that benefits humanity while mitigating potential risks.

1. **Fairness and Non-Discrimination**: Ethical AI frameworks stress the importance of fairness and ensuring that AI systems do not discriminate based on race, gender, socio-economic status, or other factors.
2. **Transparency and Explainability**: AI systems must be transparent, and their decision-making processes must be understandable. This allows users to trust AI systems and hold them accountable for their actions.
3. **Safety and Robustness**: AI systems should be safe to use, even in uncertain or unforeseen circumstances. Ethical AI frameworks advocate for comprehensive testing and risk management.

Organizational Policies for Ethical AI

1. **Internal AI Ethics Committees**: Many organizations have established internal ethics committees to evaluate AI systems' impact on society and ensure compliance with ethical standards.
2. **AI Ethics Training**: Developers should undergo training on AI ethics to understand the potential risks and ethical challenges associated with the technology.
3. **Code of Ethics for AI Development**: Establishing a clear code of ethics can guide the behavior of developers and organizations, ensuring that AI systems are designed and deployed responsibly.

Example: Implementing Ethical Guidelines in AI Development

python

```python
class EthicalAIGuidelines:
    def __init__(self, fairness, transparency, safety):
        self.fairness = fairness
        self.transparency = transparency
        self.safety = safety

    def review_guidelines(self):
        if self.fairness and self.transparency and
self.safety:
            return "Ethical guidelines are met. Proceed with
development."
        return "Review ethical guidelines for compliance."

# Usage
ethical_ai = EthicalAIGuidelines(fairness=True,
transparency=True, safety=True)
print(ethical_ai.review_guidelines())
```

- This example demonstrates how an organization can review its AI systems against ethical guidelines, ensuring compliance with fairness, transparency, and safety standards.

Navigating the legal and regulatory landscape of AI is crucial for developers to ensure that LLM agents and other AI systems are deployed ethically, responsibly, and legally. By understanding and implementing the appropriate regulations, intellectual property protections, liability considerations, and ethical frameworks, developers can contribute to the responsible evolution of AI. This chapter has highlighted the importance of navigating AI regulations, protecting innovations, managing liability, and implementing robust ethical AI frameworks to guide the development and deployment of AI technologies. By addressing these considerations, developers can help ensure that AI technologies provide value to society while minimizing risks.

Chapter 16: Emerging Technologies and Their Impact on LLM Agents

As the landscape of technology rapidly evolves, new innovations are emerging that will have a profound impact on Large Language Models (LLMs) and their capabilities. In this chapter, we explore three cutting-edge technologies—**Internet of Things (IoT)**, **Blockchain**, and **Quantum Computing**—and how they are shaping the future of LLM agents. These technologies not only enhance the performance of LLM agents but also open up new possibilities for applications in various domains. We will explore the integration of LLM agents with IoT devices, the potential of Blockchain in decentralizing AI, and the future of AI in the realm of quantum computing.

1. Integration with Internet of Things (IoT)

The **Internet of Things (IoT)** refers to the interconnected network of physical devices, vehicles, and appliances embedded with sensors, software, and other technologies that allow them to collect and exchange data. As IoT devices proliferate, their integration with LLM agents will create powerful synergies for smart systems capable of making real-time, data-driven decisions.

Smart Device Interactions

LLM agents can play a critical role in managing and interpreting the vast amounts of data generated by IoT devices. By integrating LLM agents with IoT networks, systems can become smarter, more adaptive, and capable of making decisions based on contextual information.

1. **Voice-Activated Smart Devices**: LLM agents are already at the heart of voice assistants like Amazon Alexa and Google Assistant. These devices are powered by LLMs, which help them understand and respond to natural language commands. As IoT devices become more ubiquitous, LLM agents will enable seamless interactions with a growing number of smart devices in homes, offices, and industrial environments.
2. **Context-Aware Systems**: By integrating LLM agents with IoT networks, devices can become context-aware. For example, an LLM agent in a smart home can analyze data from motion sensors,

temperature sensors, and user preferences to adjust the lighting and heating automatically, optimizing comfort and energy usage.

Example: LLM Integration with Smart Home IoT Devices

python

```python
class SmartHomeAssistant:
    def __init__(self):
        self.devices = {
            'living_room_lights': 'off',
            'thermostat': '22C',
            'security_system': 'armed'
        }

    def interact(self, command):
        if "turn on lights" in command:
            self.devices['living_room_lights'] = 'on'
        elif "adjust thermostat" in command:
            temp = command.split()[-2]  # Simple temp
extraction logic
            self.devices['thermostat'] = f'{temp}C'
        elif "disarm security" in command:
            self.devices['security_system'] = 'disarmed'

        return f"System updated: {self.devices}"

# Usage
assistant = SmartHomeAssistant()
print(assistant.interact("turn on lights"))
print(assistant.interact("adjust thermostat to 20"))
```

In this example, an LLM-based smart home assistant manages various IoT devices by interpreting natural language commands and adjusting device states accordingly.

Real-Time Data Processing

Real-time data processing is a crucial aspect of IoT, as IoT devices generate continuous streams of data that must be processed and acted upon immediately. LLM agents can provide real-time analysis of IoT data, enabling quick decision-making based on the current context.

1. **Real-Time Monitoring**: For instance, LLM agents can monitor environmental sensors in smart factories, alerting operators if unusual

conditions (such as temperature spikes or equipment malfunctions) are detected.

2. **Automated Actions**: In industrial IoT applications, LLM agents can analyze data from machines and trigger automated maintenance requests or shut down equipment to prevent damage.

Example: Real-Time IoT Data Processing with LLM

python

```python
class IoTMonitor:
    def __init__(self):
        self.devices = {'machine_1': 72, 'machine_2': 68}

    def monitor_device(self, device, temperature):
        self.devices[device] = temperature
        if temperature > 75:
            return f"Warning: {device} temperature exceeds
safe limits. Triggering maintenance."
        return f"{device} is operating within safe limits."

# Usage
monitor = IoTMonitor()
print(monitor.monitor_device('machine_1', 76))  # Exceeds
limit
```

This example shows how an LLM agent monitors the temperature of IoT devices and can take immediate action if the data indicates a problem.

Case Studies: Smart Homes, Industrial IoT Applications

- **Smart Homes**: As LLMs become more integrated with IoT devices in smart homes, homeowners will experience seamless automation, where voice commands can control everything from lighting and temperature to security systems. The LLM agent processes data from sensors and user inputs to optimize the environment based on individual preferences.
- **Industrial IoT**: In industrial settings, IoT sensors track machine health, environmental conditions, and production outputs. LLM agents integrated with these sensors can automate maintenance scheduling, optimize production processes, and enhance safety by predicting equipment failures before they occur.

2. Blockchain and Decentralized AI

Blockchain technology, with its decentralized, transparent, and secure nature, offers new opportunities for LLM agents, especially in terms of enhancing security, transparency, and data integrity.

Enhancing Security and Transparency

Blockchain can improve the security of LLM-based systems by providing an immutable ledger of all actions taken by the AI system. This is particularly important for applications in sensitive industries, such as finance, healthcare, and legal sectors, where traceability and accountability are essential.

1. **Decentralized Data Storage**: Blockchain can be used to store data in a decentralized manner, ensuring that no single entity has control over the data, which is particularly important in preventing data manipulation or unauthorized access.
2. **Smart Contracts**: Blockchain's smart contract functionality can be used to automate agreements between parties, ensuring that LLM agents execute tasks (such as transactions or data sharing) only when predefined conditions are met.

Example: Blockchain for Smart Contracts with LLMs

```python
from web3 import Web3

# Connect to Ethereum blockchain
web3 =
Web3(Web3.HTTPProvider('https://mainnet.infura.io/v3/YOUR_INF
URA_PROJECT_ID'))

# Example smart contract code (simplified for demonstration)
contract_address = '0xYourSmartContractAddress'
abi = '[...]'  # Smart contract ABI

# Interacting with smart contract
contract = web3.eth.contract(address=contract_address,
abi=abi)

def trigger_contract_action(user_address):
    tx_hash =
contract.functions.executeAction(user_address).transact()
    receipt = web3.eth.waitForTransactionReceipt(tx_hash)
    return receipt
```

```python
# Usage
user_address = '0xUserAddress'
print(trigger_contract_action(user_address))
```

In this example, an LLM agent can interact with a smart contract on the blockchain, automating certain actions when conditions are met, such as releasing funds or triggering a service.

Decentralized Decision-Making

Blockchain enables decentralized decision-making, where no single party controls the decision-making process. This decentralization is ideal for applications where multiple stakeholders need to collaborate without relying on a central authority.

1. **Decentralized AI**: LLM agents can participate in decentralized AI models where multiple nodes (or parties) contribute data and computational resources. Blockchain ensures that all participants can trust the model's outcomes without the need for a central authority.
2. **Voting and Governance**: Blockchain can be used in systems where LLM agents participate in decentralized governance models, allowing users to vote on decisions or contribute to the development of AI algorithms.

Example: Decentralized Voting with Blockchain

python

```python
class BlockchainVoting:
    def __init__(self):
        self.votes = []

    def vote(self, candidate):
        self.votes.append(candidate)
        return f"Vote for {candidate} recorded."

    def tally_votes(self):
        return {candidate: self.votes.count(candidate) for
candidate in set(self.votes)}

# Usage
voting_system = BlockchainVoting()
print(voting_system.vote("Candidate A"))
print(voting_system.vote("Candidate B"))
print(voting_system.tally_votes())
```

This simplified example shows how blockchain can be used in decentralized voting systems, where LLM agents can record and tally votes securely.

Potential Use Cases and Implementations

1. **Supply Chain Management**: Blockchain can ensure transparency in supply chains, where LLM agents monitor and verify every step of the process.
2. **Healthcare Data Exchange**: In healthcare, blockchain can securely store medical records, and LLM agents can help analyze and make recommendations based on that data while ensuring privacy and compliance.

---

3. Quantum Computing and AI

Quantum computing, a revolutionary technology that leverages the principles of quantum mechanics, has the potential to significantly enhance the processing power of AI systems, including LLM agents. Quantum computers can solve certain problems that classical computers struggle with, especially in tasks that require vast amounts of computational power.

Potential Enhancements in Processing Power

Quantum computing promises to enhance the computational power of LLM agents by enabling them to process and analyze data exponentially faster than classical computers. With quantum algorithms, tasks that would typically take years on current hardware could be completed in seconds or minutes.

1. **Parallel Processing**: Quantum computers can perform many calculations simultaneously, making them well-suited for training large-scale AI models that require significant computational resources.
2. **Optimization Problems**: Quantum computing could significantly enhance optimization algorithms used in machine learning, improving the training efficiency of LLMs.

Example: Quantum Computing for Optimization Problems

```python
```

```
# Example of Quantum Optimization using Qiskit (IBM's quantum
computing SDK)
from qiskit import QuantumCircuit, Aer, execute

# Create a simple quantum circuit
qc = QuantumCircuit(2)
qc.h(0)  # Hadamard gate on qubit 0
qc.cx(0, 1)  # CNOT gate between qubits 0 and 1

# Simulate the quantum circuit
simulator = Aer.get_backend('statevector_simulator')
result = execute(qc, simulator).result()

# Get the quantum state
state = result.get_statevector(qc, decimals=3)
print("Quantum state:", state)
```

- This example uses **Qiskit**, IBM's quantum computing SDK, to create and simulate a basic quantum circuit. Quantum computers can help optimize complex AI models and computations.

Future Prospects for Quantum AI Agents

Quantum AI holds immense potential for fields like drug discovery, materials science, and AI model training. By leveraging quantum algorithms, LLM agents could analyze complex datasets much more efficiently, enabling breakthroughs in various scientific and technological domains.

Current Developments and Milestones

While quantum computing is still in its early stages, significant progress has been made in terms of quantum hardware and algorithms. Leading tech companies, such as IBM, Google, and Microsoft, have demonstrated successful quantum algorithms, and specialized quantum processors are becoming more widely available.

Example: Quantum Machine Learning

```python
from qiskit_machine_learning.algorithms import QSVM
from qiskit_machine_learning.datasets import wine

# Use Qiskit for a quantum support vector machine
data, labels = wine(training_size=20, test_size=10)
```

```
svm = QSVM()
svm.fit(data, labels)
print(svm.score(data, labels))
```

- This example uses Qiskit's machine learning library to implement a Quantum Support Vector Machine (QSVM) for classification tasks, demonstrating how quantum computing can enhance machine learning models.

The integration of emerging technologies such as IoT, blockchain, and quantum computing with LLM agents holds the potential to revolutionize various industries. By enabling smarter device interactions, decentralized decision-making, and enhancing processing capabilities, these technologies are setting the stage for the next generation of AI applications. As LLM agents continue to evolve, their synergy with these cutting-edge technologies will unlock new possibilities, driving innovation and improving efficiencies across a wide range of sectors.

Chapter 17: Advances in Natural Language Processing and Understanding

Natural Language Processing (NLP) has made tremendous strides in recent years, with advancements driving the development of sophisticated systems that understand, generate, and interact using human language. The evolution of NLP techniques has brought deeper levels of comprehension, better conversational management, and enhanced multilingual capabilities. This chapter explores the latest advancements in NLP and how they are being applied to Large Language Models (LLMs) and conversational AI agents. We will cover three key areas of progress: contextual and semantic understanding, conversational AI enhancements, and multilingual capabilities. Each section will discuss how these advancements improve LLM agents and contribute to more natural, accurate, and effective AI-human interactions.

---

1. Contextual and Semantic Understanding

Deepening Language Comprehension

Traditional NLP models focused on understanding individual words or phrases in isolation, which limited their ability to process more complex language constructs like idioms, metaphors, and polysemy (words with multiple meanings). Advances in LLMs have shifted this approach to one that emphasizes **contextual understanding**, allowing models to interpret language based on the broader context in which it appears.

Contextual understanding involves recognizing the meaning of words not just in isolation, but in relation to the surrounding text or conversation. LLMs such as GPT-3 and GPT-4 use attention mechanisms to process and understand long-range dependencies in text, enabling them to interpret more complex relationships between words.

Key Concepts:

1. **Attention Mechanism**: This mechanism allows models to focus on relevant parts of a sentence or passage when generating output, improving their ability to understand complex contexts.
2. **Transformers**: Transformer models, which form the backbone of many modern LLMs, rely on self-attention to learn relationships between words in different parts of a sentence, even if they are far apart.

Example: Contextual Understanding with Transformers

```
from transformers import pipeline

# Using a pre-trained BERT model for contextual language
understanding
nlp = pipeline("fill-mask", model="bert-base-uncased")

sentence = "The man went to the [MASK] to buy some
groceries."
output = nlp(sentence)
print(output)
```

- In this example, the BERT model fills in the missing word ("store") based on its understanding of the context, demonstrating how transformers process context to infer missing information.

Handling Ambiguities and Nuances

Human language is rich with ambiguities—words and phrases that can have multiple meanings depending on the context. LLMs have made significant progress in handling these ambiguities, enabling them to provide more accurate and nuanced interpretations.

1. **Polysemy**: Words like "bank" can refer to a financial institution or the side of a river, depending on context. LLMs leverage large-scale data and contextual clues to resolve these ambiguities.
2. **Pragmatics**: Pragmatics refers to how language is used in practice, including how speakers convey meaning beyond the literal words. LLMs are increasingly able to grasp these subtleties, improving their ability to engage in natural, human-like conversation.

Example: Disambiguating Polysemy

```python
from transformers import pipeline

# Using a pre-trained GPT model to understand the word "bank"
nlp = pipeline("text-generation", model="gpt-2")

sentence_1 = "She deposited money into the bank."
sentence_2 = "The boat was moored by the river bank."

output_1 = nlp(sentence_1)
output_2 = nlp(sentence_2)

print(f"Output 1: {output_1[0]['generated_text']}")
print(f"Output 2: {output_2[0]['generated_text']}")
```

- In this case, GPT-2 uses its contextual understanding to determine the appropriate meaning of "bank" based on the surrounding text.

---

2. Conversational AI Enhancements

Multi-Turn Dialogue Management

A significant challenge in conversational AI is managing **multi-turn dialogue**, where the conversation spans multiple exchanges, and context must be maintained over time. Unlike single-turn interactions (e.g., "What's the weather like today?"), multi-turn dialogue involves handling dynamic conversations with back-and-forth exchanges. An effective conversational AI system must remember previous interactions and incorporate this context into future responses.

Advancements in LLMs have enabled better memory and tracking of conversational state, allowing models to handle more natural and coherent multi-turn dialogues. The incorporation of **state management** and **dialogue history tracking** ensures that AI agents provide relevant and contextually appropriate responses.

Key Concepts:

1. **Contextual Memory**: Modern LLMs can store context across multiple turns, enabling them to understand the flow of a conversation.

2. **Dialogue History**: By retaining the history of the conversation, LLM agents can adapt their responses to follow up on earlier topics, ask clarifying questions, and maintain continuity.

Example: Multi-Turn Dialogue Management

```
from transformers import pipeline

# Create a conversational pipeline for managing multi-turn
dialogue
nlp = pipeline("conversational", model="microsoft/DialoGPT-
medium")

conversation = "Hello, how are you?"
response = nlp(conversation)
print(response)

conversation = "What's the weather like today?"
response = nlp(conversation)
print(response)
```

- This example demonstrates how the model handles multi-turn dialogue by responding appropriately to each question, with the potential to integrate contextual memory for more complex conversations.

Emotion and Sentiment Analysis

Emotion and sentiment analysis is another key enhancement in conversational AI. Understanding emotions (e.g., happiness, frustration, sadness) allows conversational agents to tailor responses more empathetically, improving user experience.

1. **Sentiment Analysis**: This involves determining whether the sentiment expressed in a text is positive, negative, or neutral. More advanced models can recognize nuanced sentiments, like sarcasm or mixed emotions.
2. **Emotion Detection**: This goes beyond sentiment to identify specific emotions, such as joy, anger, or sadness, and tailor responses accordingly.

Example: Emotion and Sentiment Analysis

```
from transformers import pipeline
```

```
# Create a sentiment analysis pipeline
nlp = pipeline("sentiment-analysis")

text = "I am really excited about this new AI technology!"
output = nlp(text)
print(output)

text2 = "I am feeling a bit frustrated with this system."
output2 = nlp(text2)
print(output2)
```

- This example uses a sentiment analysis pipeline to determine the sentiment of a given text, enabling the conversational AI to adjust its responses based on the user's emotional state.

---

3. Multilingual and Cross-Cultural Capabilities

Building Globally Applicable Agents

One of the most exciting advancements in NLP is the ability to build **multilingual and cross-cultural** agents that can serve users from different linguistic backgrounds and cultural contexts. Traditional NLP models were often limited to English or a few major languages, but the development of multilingual models like mBERT and XLM-R has enabled LLM agents to understand and generate text in many languages, making them suitable for global applications.

Key Concepts:

1. **Multilingual Models**: These models are trained on datasets containing multiple languages, enabling them to process and generate text across different linguistic systems.
2. **Cross-Cultural Adaptation**: Beyond language, LLMs can be adapted to handle cultural differences in communication styles, humor, and context.

Example: Multilingual Text Generation

```
from transformers import pipeline

# Create a multilingual text generation pipeline
nlp = pipeline("text-generation", model="gpt-2")
```

```
text = "Bonjour, comment ça va?"  # French greeting
response = nlp(text)
print(response)

text2 = "Hola, ¿cómo estás?"  # Spanish greeting
response2 = nlp(text2)
print(response2)
```

- This example shows how a multilingual LLM agent can generate responses in different languages, making it adaptable to various regions and users.

Overcoming Language Barriers

Language barriers have historically been a significant challenge in global communication. LLM agents equipped with multilingual capabilities can help bridge these gaps by offering real-time translation and interpretation services, fostering better communication across different languages and cultures.

1. **Real-Time Translation**: LLM agents can provide real-time translation for text, voice, and even video, allowing users to converse seamlessly in different languages.
2. **Cultural Context**: These agents can be designed to recognize cultural norms and adapt responses to reflect local customs, ensuring that communication remains appropriate and respectful.

Example: Language Translation with LLM

```
from transformers import MarianMTModel, MarianTokenizer

# Load a translation model (English to French)
model_name = 'Helsinki-NLP/opus-mt-en-fr'
model = MarianMTModel.from_pretrained(model_name)
tokenizer = MarianTokenizer.from_pretrained(model_name)

# Translate text
text = "Hello, how are you?"
tokens = tokenizer(text, return_tensors="pt")
translation = model.generate(**tokens)
translated_text = tokenizer.decode(translation[0],
skip_special_tokens=True)
print(f"Translated Text: {translated_text}")
```

- In this example, the LLM agent translates English text into French using a pre-trained MarianMT model, demonstrating the potential of LLM agents to overcome language barriers in real-time.

The advancements in Natural Language Processing (NLP) and understanding have led to the development of more capable, responsive, and globally applicable Large Language Model (LLM) agents. From contextual comprehension to multilingual capabilities, these improvements are transforming the way LLM agents interact with humans. Enhanced conversational AI, including better management of multi-turn dialogues and sentiment analysis, makes LLM agents more empathetic and contextually aware. Moreover, the ability to understand and communicate in multiple languages opens up new possibilities for global applications.

As LLMs continue to evolve, their integration with emerging technologies will further enhance their capabilities, enabling them to better serve users in diverse cultural, linguistic, and emotional contexts. These advancements are paving the way for more intelligent, adaptive, and universally accessible AI systems.

Chapter 17: Advances in Natural Language Processing and Understanding

Natural Language Processing (NLP) has made tremendous strides in recent years, with advancements driving the development of sophisticated systems that understand, generate, and interact using human language. The evolution of NLP techniques has brought deeper levels of comprehension, better conversational management, and enhanced multilingual capabilities. This chapter explores the latest advancements in NLP and how they are being applied to Large Language Models (LLMs) and conversational AI agents. We will cover three key areas of progress: contextual and semantic understanding, conversational AI enhancements, and multilingual capabilities. Each section will discuss how these advancements improve LLM agents and contribute to more natural, accurate, and effective AI-human interactions.

---

1. Contextual and Semantic Understanding

Deepening Language Comprehension

Traditional NLP models focused on understanding individual words or phrases in isolation, which limited their ability to process more complex language constructs like idioms, metaphors, and polysemy (words with multiple meanings). Advances in LLMs have shifted this approach to one that emphasizes **contextual understanding**, allowing models to interpret language based on the broader context in which it appears.

Contextual understanding involves recognizing the meaning of words not just in isolation, but in relation to the surrounding text or conversation. LLMs such as GPT-3 and GPT-4 use attention mechanisms to process and understand long-range dependencies in text, enabling them to interpret more complex relationships between words.

Key Concepts:

1. **Attention Mechanism**: This mechanism allows models to focus on relevant parts of a sentence or passage when generating output, improving their ability to understand complex contexts.
2. **Transformers**: Transformer models, which form the backbone of many modern LLMs, rely on self-attention to learn relationships between words in different parts of a sentence, even if they are far apart.

Example: Contextual Understanding with Transformers

```python
from transformers import pipeline

# Using a pre-trained BERT model for contextual language
understanding
nlp = pipeline("fill-mask", model="bert-base-uncased")

sentence = "The man went to the [MASK] to buy some
groceries."
output = nlp(sentence)
print(output)
```

- In this example, the BERT model fills in the missing word ("store") based on its understanding of the context, demonstrating how transformers process context to infer missing information.

Handling Ambiguities and Nuances

Human language is rich with ambiguities—words and phrases that can have multiple meanings depending on the context. LLMs have made significant progress in handling these ambiguities, enabling them to provide more accurate and nuanced interpretations.

1. **Polysemy**: Words like "bank" can refer to a financial institution or the side of a river, depending on context. LLMs leverage large-scale data and contextual clues to resolve these ambiguities.
2. **Pragmatics**: Pragmatics refers to how language is used in practice, including how speakers convey meaning beyond the literal words. LLMs are increasingly able to grasp these subtleties, improving their ability to engage in natural, human-like conversation.

Example: Disambiguating Polysemy

```python
from transformers import pipeline

# Using a pre-trained GPT model to understand the word "bank"
nlp = pipeline("text-generation", model="gpt-2")

sentence_1 = "She deposited money into the bank."
sentence_2 = "The boat was moored by the river bank."

output_1 = nlp(sentence_1)
output_2 = nlp(sentence_2)

print(f"Output 1: {output_1[0]['generated_text']}")
print(f"Output 2: {output_2[0]['generated_text']}")
```

- In this case, GPT-2 uses its contextual understanding to determine the appropriate meaning of "bank" based on the surrounding text.

---

2. Conversational AI Enhancements

Multi-Turn Dialogue Management

A significant challenge in conversational AI is managing **multi-turn dialogue**, where the conversation spans multiple exchanges, and context must be maintained over time. Unlike single-turn interactions (e.g., "What's the weather like today?"), multi-turn dialogue involves handling dynamic conversations with back-and-forth exchanges. An effective conversational AI system must remember previous interactions and incorporate this context into future responses.

Advancements in LLMs have enabled better memory and tracking of conversational state, allowing models to handle more natural and coherent multi-turn dialogues. The incorporation of **state management** and **dialogue history tracking** ensures that AI agents provide relevant and contextually appropriate responses.

Key Concepts:

1. **Contextual Memory**: Modern LLMs can store context across multiple turns, enabling them to understand the flow of a conversation.

2. **Dialogue History**: By retaining the history of the conversation, LLM agents can adapt their responses to follow up on earlier topics, ask clarifying questions, and maintain continuity.

Example: Multi-Turn Dialogue Management

```
from transformers import pipeline

# Create a conversational pipeline for managing multi-turn
dialogue
nlp = pipeline("conversational", model="microsoft/DialoGPT-
medium")

conversation = "Hello, how are you?"
response = nlp(conversation)
print(response)

conversation = "What's the weather like today?"
response = nlp(conversation)
print(response)
```

- This example demonstrates how the model handles multi-turn dialogue by responding appropriately to each question, with the potential to integrate contextual memory for more complex conversations.

Emotion and Sentiment Analysis

Emotion and sentiment analysis is another key enhancement in conversational AI. Understanding emotions (e.g., happiness, frustration, sadness) allows conversational agents to tailor responses more empathetically, improving user experience.

1. **Sentiment Analysis**: This involves determining whether the sentiment expressed in a text is positive, negative, or neutral. More advanced models can recognize nuanced sentiments, like sarcasm or mixed emotions.
2. **Emotion Detection**: This goes beyond sentiment to identify specific emotions, such as joy, anger, or sadness, and tailor responses accordingly.

Example: Emotion and Sentiment Analysis

```
from transformers import pipeline
```

```
# Create a sentiment analysis pipeline
nlp = pipeline("sentiment-analysis")

text = "I am really excited about this new AI technology!"
output = nlp(text)
print(output)

text2 = "I am feeling a bit frustrated with this system."
output2 = nlp(text2)
print(output2)
```

- This example uses a sentiment analysis pipeline to determine the sentiment of a given text, enabling the conversational AI to adjust its responses based on the user's emotional state.

---

3. Multilingual and Cross-Cultural Capabilities

Building Globally Applicable Agents

One of the most exciting advancements in NLP is the ability to build **multilingual and cross-cultural** agents that can serve users from different linguistic backgrounds and cultural contexts. Traditional NLP models were often limited to English or a few major languages, but the development of multilingual models like mBERT and XLM-R has enabled LLM agents to understand and generate text in many languages, making them suitable for global applications.

Key Concepts:

1. **Multilingual Models**: These models are trained on datasets containing multiple languages, enabling them to process and generate text across different linguistic systems.
2. **Cross-Cultural Adaptation**: Beyond language, LLMs can be adapted to handle cultural differences in communication styles, humor, and context.

Example: Multilingual Text Generation

```
from transformers import pipeline

# Create a multilingual text generation pipeline
nlp = pipeline("text-generation", model="gpt-2")
```

```
text = "Bonjour, comment ça va?"  # French greeting
response = nlp(text)
print(response)

text2 = "Hola, ¿cómo estás?"  # Spanish greeting
response2 = nlp(text2)
print(response2)
```

- This example shows how a multilingual LLM agent can generate responses in different languages, making it adaptable to various regions and users.

Overcoming Language Barriers

Language barriers have historically been a significant challenge in global communication. LLM agents equipped with multilingual capabilities can help bridge these gaps by offering real-time translation and interpretation services, fostering better communication across different languages and cultures.

1. **Real-Time Translation**: LLM agents can provide real-time translation for text, voice, and even video, allowing users to converse seamlessly in different languages.
2. **Cultural Context**: These agents can be designed to recognize cultural norms and adapt responses to reflect local customs, ensuring that communication remains appropriate and respectful.

Example: Language Translation with LLM

```
from transformers import MarianMTModel, MarianTokenizer

# Load a translation model (English to French)
model_name = 'Helsinki-NLP/opus-mt-en-fr'
model = MarianMTModel.from_pretrained(model_name)
tokenizer = MarianTokenizer.from_pretrained(model_name)

# Translate text
text = "Hello, how are you?"
tokens = tokenizer(text, return_tensors="pt")
translation = model.generate(**tokens)
translated_text = tokenizer.decode(translation[0],
skip_special_tokens=True)
print(f"Translated Text: {translated_text}")
```

- In this example, the LLM agent translates English text into French using a pre-trained MarianMT model, demonstrating the potential of LLM agents to overcome language barriers in real-time.

The advancements in Natural Language Processing (NLP) and understanding have led to the development of more capable, responsive, and globally applicable Large Language Model (LLM) agents. From contextual comprehension to multilingual capabilities, these improvements are transforming the way LLM agents interact with humans. Enhanced conversational AI, including better management of multi-turn dialogues and sentiment analysis, makes LLM agents more empathetic and contextually aware. Moreover, the ability to understand and communicate in multiple languages opens up new possibilities for global applications.

As LLMs continue to evolve, their integration with emerging technologies will further enhance their capabilities, enabling them to better serve users in diverse cultural, linguistic, and emotional contexts. These advancements are paving the way for more intelligent, adaptive, and universally accessible AI systems.

Chapter 18: Long-Term Implications for Society and Industry

The rapid development and deployment of Artificial Intelligence (AI), particularly in the form of Large Language Models (LLMs) and autonomous systems, is shaping the future of society and industry. While the benefits of AI are significant, there are also important long-term implications that need to be carefully considered. This chapter explores the potential impact of AI on the future of work, social dynamics, and economic transformations. By understanding these changes, we can better prepare for the societal shifts that AI will bring.

1. AI and the Future of Work

Automation of Jobs

AI technologies, including LLMs and autonomous systems, are increasingly capable of performing tasks that traditionally required human intervention. This trend is expected to accelerate, leading to automation in a wide range of industries, from manufacturing to services. The potential for AI to replace human labor has sparked discussions about the future of work and the impact on employment.

Key Points:

1. **Automation of Routine and Repetitive Tasks**: Many jobs that involve repetitive, rule-based tasks are particularly susceptible to automation. For example, data entry, administrative tasks, and basic customer service functions can be efficiently performed by AI agents, freeing up human workers to focus on higher-level tasks.
2. **Impact on Blue-Collar and White-Collar Jobs**: AI is expected to affect both blue-collar jobs (e.g., factory workers, truck drivers) and white-collar jobs (e.g., legal assistants, paralegals, customer service representatives). While automation could lead to job displacement in these areas, it also presents opportunities for creating new roles.

Example: Automating Routine Administrative Tasks

```
import pandas as pd
```

```python
# Simulating data processing automation
data = pd.DataFrame({
    'name': ['Alice', 'Bob', 'Charlie'],
    'address': ['123 Main St', '456 Oak St', '789 Pine St'],
    'phone_number': ['555-1234', '555-5678', '555-8765']
})

# Automatically cleaning up data by removing sensitive
information
data_cleaned = data.drop(columns=['phone_number'])

print("Cleaned Data:\n", data_cleaned)
```

- In this example, a routine administrative task like cleaning up a dataset can be automated by LLMs, allowing human employees to focus on more strategic activities.

New Opportunities and Skill Requirements

While automation may displace certain jobs, it will also create new opportunities and require a shift in skillsets. Workers will need to adapt by acquiring new skills that complement AI technologies and take advantage of the opportunities created by automation.

1. **AI Development and Maintenance**: As AI systems become more integrated into industries, there will be an increasing demand for skilled workers in AI development, maintenance, and ethical oversight. Data scientists, AI engineers, and machine learning specialists will play crucial roles in shaping the future workforce.
2. **Human-AI Collaboration**: Rather than replacing humans entirely, AI is likely to augment human capabilities, enabling workers to focus on more creative, strategic, and high-level tasks. For instance, doctors may rely on AI to help with diagnostics, but the final treatment decisions will still require human judgment.

Example: Training AI for New Opportunities

```python
# Simulate a skill-building course for data scientists
def create_skill_course(course_name, course_duration):
    return f"{course_name} - Duration: {course_duration}
hours"

# Example course for AI training
course = create_skill_course("AI for Healthcare", 40)
print(course)
```

- This example demonstrates how specialized training courses, like AI for healthcare, can be developed to help workers acquire the skills needed to operate in an AI-enhanced world.

---

2. Social Impacts of Autonomous Systems

Changes in Human Interaction

The increasing prevalence of autonomous systems, including LLM agents and robots, will fundamentally change how humans interact with technology, with each other, and with the world around them. As AI agents become more capable of carrying out tasks autonomously, human roles in these processes may shift, leading to changes in social dynamics.

1. **Human-AI Interaction**: The way we interact with machines will evolve. As AI systems become more intelligent and conversational, humans will interact with them in ways that resemble human-to-human communication. This could lead to more personalized and efficient interactions, but it also raises questions about the emotional and psychological effects of such interactions.
2. **Social Isolation vs. Social Connectivity**: On the one hand, AI could facilitate deeper social connections by enabling remote communication and providing companionship, particularly for vulnerable populations like the elderly. On the other hand, excessive reliance on AI could contribute to social isolation, as people might become more accustomed to interacting with machines than with other humans.

Example: AI-Assisted Social Interaction

```python
class SocialAI:
    def __init__(self, user_name):
        self.user_name = user_name

    def greet(self):
        return f"Hello {self.user_name}, how can I assist you today?"

# Usage
ai_assistant = SocialAI("Alice")
print(ai_assistant.greet())
```

- In this example, an AI agent interacts with users in a social context, demonstrating how AI systems can foster communication and assist in personal interactions.

Addressing Ethical Dilemmas

As autonomous systems become more capable, they may be placed in situations where ethical dilemmas arise. For instance, an autonomous car might need to decide how to respond in a life-threatening situation, or a healthcare AI might need to make decisions about patient care. These situations raise important questions about accountability and ethics.

1. **Ethical Decision-Making**: Developers must build ethical guidelines into AI systems to ensure that they make decisions aligned with societal values. This includes establishing frameworks for fairness, transparency, and accountability in decision-making processes.
2. **Bias and Discrimination**: AI systems, including LLM agents, may inherit biases from the data used to train them. Ensuring that AI systems do not perpetuate or exacerbate social biases is a key ethical challenge.

Example: Ethical Decision-Making in AI

```
class AutonomousVehicle:
    def __init__(self, decision_outcome):
        self.decision_outcome = decision_outcome

    def make_decision(self):
        if self.decision_outcome == "crash":
            return "The car will take action to minimize
harm."
        else:
            return "The car will continue on its path
safely."

# Usage
vehicle = AutonomousVehicle("crash")
print(vehicle.make_decision())
```

- This simple example demonstrates an autonomous vehicle making an ethical decision to minimize harm in the event of an unavoidable crash.

3. Economic and Industrial Transformations

Disruption of Traditional Industries

AI and automation are disrupting traditional industries by transforming how goods and services are produced, delivered, and consumed. Many industries are undergoing radical changes, driven by the increased efficiency, cost-effectiveness, and scalability of AI technologies.

1. **Manufacturing and Production**: Robotics and AI-powered automation are transforming manufacturing processes, improving productivity, reducing costs, and enabling mass customization. Smart factories, powered by AI and IoT, are revolutionizing how products are designed, produced, and distributed.
2. **Retail and Customer Service**: AI is reshaping the retail industry by enhancing customer experiences through personalized recommendations, virtual shopping assistants, and automated inventory management. Traditional retail jobs may be replaced by AI-driven solutions that offer faster, more efficient services.

Example: AI-Powered Manufacturing

```
class SmartFactory:
    def __init__(self, product_line):
        self.product_line = product_line

    def automate_production(self):
        return f"Automating production of {self.product_line}
using AI-powered robots."

# Usage
factory = SmartFactory("electronics")
print(factory.automate_production())
```

- This example illustrates how AI-powered systems can automate production in smart factories, driving efficiencies and transforming traditional manufacturing.

Growth of AI-Driven Sectors

While AI disrupts traditional industries, it also creates entirely new sectors driven by AI technologies. As businesses and organizations embrace AI, new markets and opportunities are emerging, particularly in areas like AI development, data analytics, and AI-enabled services.

1. **AI Services and Consulting**: Companies specializing in AI development, deployment, and consulting are rapidly growing. These firms provide expertise in creating tailored AI solutions for businesses across various industries, from healthcare to finance.
2. **Data Science and Analytics**: The demand for data scientists, machine learning engineers, and AI specialists is increasing as organizations seek to leverage data to gain a competitive edge. AI-driven analytics platforms are empowering businesses to make data-driven decisions at scale.

Example: AI Services and Consulting

```python
class AIConsulting:
    def __init__(self, client_name, service_type):
        self.client_name = client_name
        self.service_type = service_type

    def provide_service(self):
        return f"Providing {self.service_type} to
{self.client_name}."

# Usage
consulting = AIConsulting("TechCorp", "AI-driven analytics")
print(consulting.provide_service())
```

- This example shows how AI services, like consulting for AI-driven analytics, can provide valuable support to businesses as they integrate AI into their operations.

The long-term implications of AI, particularly in the form of LLM agents and autonomous systems, are profound and far-reaching. From the transformation of the workforce and social interactions to the disruption of traditional industries and the emergence of new AI-driven sectors, AI will continue to reshape society in ways both exciting and challenging. As we move forward, it is essential to ensure that these technologies are developed and deployed responsibly, with a focus on maximizing benefits while minimizing risks. By understanding these implications, society and industry can better prepare for the AI-powered future that lies ahead.

Chapter 19: Designing User-Centric LLM Agents

In this chapter, we explore the crucial aspect of designing **user-centric** Large Language Model (LLM) agents. As LLMs become more integrated into a wide array of applications—from virtual assistants to customer service bots and healthcare advisors—the user experience (UX) plays a pivotal role in determining the effectiveness of these systems. A well-designed LLM agent not only delivers accurate and helpful responses but also engages users in an intuitive and meaningful way. By focusing on UX principles, interaction design, and continuous evaluation, we can ensure that LLM agents are both user-friendly and efficient.

1. Principles of UX Design in AI

User experience (UX) design is the process of creating products that provide meaningful and relevant experiences to users. In the context of LLM agents, this means designing interfaces and interactions that are easy to use, efficient, and pleasant while ensuring that the technology aligns with users' needs and goals.

Key UX Principles for LLM Agents:

1. **Simplicity and Clarity**:
    o   An LLM agent should present information clearly and concisely. Complex language, ambiguous responses, or unnecessary details can confuse the user and hinder their experience. Striving for simplicity in both the agent's responses and its overall design is essential.
    o   Example: When responding to a user's query, avoid overly technical jargon unless explicitly requested.
2. **Consistency**:
    o   Consistency in responses, visual design, and interaction patterns helps users understand how to interact with the agent. It makes the system feel more predictable and easier to navigate.
    o   Example: The tone of the conversation should remain consistent, whether the agent is being formal or casual.
3. **User Control and Freedom**:

o Users should feel in control of their interactions with LLM agents. They should be able to easily correct mistakes, change direction, or end conversations without feeling trapped.

o Example: Allowing users to easily undo or rephrase a previous action (e.g., "I didn't mean that, please try again") improves their confidence in using the system.

4. **Error Prevention and Recovery**:

o Proactively preventing errors is better than offering solutions after the fact. LLM agents should be designed to anticipate possible user mistakes and offer helpful guidance without causing frustration.

o Example: If the user's input is ambiguous, an LLM agent can ask clarifying questions rather than making incorrect assumptions.

5. **Personalization**:

o Personalization makes the user experience more relevant. LLM agents can adapt their responses based on user preferences, previous interactions, and other context to make the conversation feel more personalized.

o Example: "I remember you like to receive updates in the morning. Would you like to hear today's news now?"

Example: Simplicity in LLM Agent Responses

```
# Simulate a simple and clear response from an LLM agent
def respond_to_query(query):
    # Simple and clear responses
    if query.lower() == "what is the weather today?":
        return "Today's weather is sunny with a high of
75°F."
    elif query.lower() == "how do I reset my password?":
        return "To reset your password, click 'Forgot
password' on the login page."
    else:
        return "I'm sorry, I didn't quite understand that."

# Example usage
user_query = "What is the weather today?"
response = respond_to_query(user_query)
print(response)
```

- In this example, the LLM agent provides clear and direct answers, making it easy for the user to understand the information they need.

2. Interaction Design for Conversational Agents

The design of interactions between users and LLM agents is fundamental to creating a positive and effective experience. Conversational AI must allow for smooth, natural exchanges that feel engaging and responsive. In this section, we dive deeper into how to design interactions that facilitate effective communication.

Key Considerations for Interaction Design:

1. **Flow and Structure of Dialogue**:
   - A well-structured conversation ensures that the user is guided smoothly through the interaction. For multi-turn dialogues, maintaining a coherent flow is critical. This means the system should keep track of the conversation's context and adapt based on previous turns.
   - Example: A chatbot assisting with booking a flight should ask for details in a logical sequence: destination, dates, number of passengers, etc., rather than jumping between unrelated topics.
2. **Natural Language Understanding (NLU)**:
   - The heart of interaction design in LLM agents lies in their ability to understand natural language inputs. A good conversational agent should be able to understand various ways in which a user might phrase a question or request, including slang, abbreviations, and typos.
   - Example: If a user asks "What's the temp today?" instead of "What is the temperature today?", the agent should still provide an accurate response.
3. **Turn-Taking and Responsiveness**:
   - Turn-taking refers to the way users and agents exchange information. An effective LLM agent listens carefully to each user input and provides timely responses. The agent should also be able to handle interruptions, pauses, and follow-up questions seamlessly.
   - Example: If a user interrupts the agent with a follow-up question ("How about tomorrow?"), the agent should pause and respond to the new query without confusion.
4. **Tone and Personality**:
   - The agent's tone and personality should align with the context of the interaction. For customer service, a polite, professional

tone might be appropriate, while a more casual, friendly tone could work for entertainment applications.
- o Example: An LLM agent in a formal business context should maintain a respectful tone, while a chatbot for a gaming site could adopt a more playful, engaging voice.

Example: Designing Dialogue Flow in an LLM Agent

```
class ConversationManager:
    def __init__(self):
        self.context = {}

    def handle_input(self, user_input):
        if 'destination' not in self.context:
            self.context['destination'] = user_input
            return "Got it! When would you like to travel?"
        elif 'dates' not in self.context:
            self.context['dates'] = user_input
            return "Perfect! How many passengers will there
be?"
        else:
            return f"Thank you for the details. You've chosen
{self.context['destination']} for {self.context['dates']}."

# Example usage
conversation = ConversationManager()
print(conversation.handle_input("Paris"))
print(conversation.handle_input("Next week"))
print(conversation.handle_input("2"))
```

- In this example, the agent asks for input in a logical sequence, capturing relevant information at each step of the conversation to complete the task (e.g., booking a flight).

---

3. Evaluating and Improving User Experience

Once an LLM agent has been deployed, continuous evaluation and improvement of the user experience are essential to ensure that the system remains relevant and effective. Regular assessments allow developers to identify pain points, refine interactions, and enhance the system's performance over time.

Techniques for Evaluating User Experience:

1. **User Feedback**:
   - Direct feedback from users is one of the most valuable sources of insight. Implementing mechanisms for users to rate their experiences or provide comments can help developers understand what works and what doesn't.
   - Example: After a conversation with a customer service agent, users could be asked, "How helpful was this interaction?" and given options like "Very helpful," "Somewhat helpful," or "Not helpful."
2. **Usability Testing**:
   - Conducting usability tests with real users can reveal issues related to the navigation, ease of use, and overall user satisfaction. These tests can involve both automated testing (e.g., using scripts to simulate user interactions) and manual testing (e.g., observing users as they interact with the agent).
   - Example: Observing a user interact with the LLM agent during a simulated scenario, such as making a purchase, can uncover unexpected behavior or confusing dialogue choices.
3. **Analytics and Performance Metrics**:
   - Collecting data on how users interact with the system (e.g., response times, user retention, conversation length) can help identify areas for improvement. Additionally, performance metrics such as accuracy, completeness of responses, and error rates provide quantitative insights into system performance.
   - Example: Tracking the number of successful task completions versus failed attempts can highlight areas where the agent needs to be improved.

Example: Gathering User Feedback and Analytics

```
class UserFeedback:
    def __init__(self):
        self.responses = []

    def collect_feedback(self, rating, comment):
        self.responses.append({'rating': rating, 'comment':
comment})
        return "Thank you for your feedback!"

    def get_analytics(self):
        return len(self.responses), sum([response['rating']
for response in self.responses]) / len(self.responses)
```

```
# Example usage
feedback = UserFeedback()
print(feedback.collect_feedback(4, "The agent was helpful,
but could be faster."))
print(feedback.get_analytics())
```

- This example collects user feedback and calculates basic analytics
  like average rating and the number of responses, helping to gauge
  user satisfaction and identify areas for improvement.

Designing user-centric LLM agents requires a deep understanding of user
experience principles, interaction design, and continuous improvement. By
focusing on simplicity, clarity, consistency, and personalization, LLM agents
can be made more accessible and enjoyable for users. Effective interaction
design, which includes managing multi-turn dialogues, understanding natural
language inputs, and incorporating a suitable tone, ensures that the agent
feels intuitive and responsive. Lastly, ongoing evaluation using user
feedback, usability testing, and performance metrics ensures that the system
remains relevant and efficient, continually enhancing the user experience. By
following these best practices, developers can build LLM agents that not
only perform their tasks but also provide a satisfying and engaging
experience for users.

Chapter 20: Troubleshooting and Maintaining LLM Agents

Building and deploying a Large Language Model (LLM) agent is a significant technical achievement, but its journey does not end once it is launched. Continuous maintenance and troubleshooting are essential to ensuring that the agent remains reliable, efficient, and effective in meeting users' needs. This chapter will cover the common issues that developers face with LLM agents, strategies for monitoring and diagnosing problems, and techniques for the continuous improvement of these systems.

1. Common Issues and Solutions

While LLM agents are designed to handle a wide range of tasks, they may experience issues related to accuracy, performance, and user experience. Addressing these issues promptly and effectively is key to maintaining a robust system.

Issue 1: Inaccurate or Irrelevant Responses

LLM agents may sometimes produce responses that are inaccurate, irrelevant, or incomplete. This issue can stem from several factors, including poor training data, a lack of contextual understanding, or the model's failure to interpret user intent properly.

Potential Causes:

- **Insufficient or Biased Training Data**: If the model was trained on unrepresentative or biased data, it may produce incorrect responses.
- **Context Loss**: In multi-turn conversations, LLM agents may lose track of the context, resulting in incoherent or irrelevant replies.
- **Ambiguity in User Queries**: If a user's query is vague or ambiguous, the model may misinterpret it and give an incorrect response.

Solutions:

1. **Improving Training Data**: Ensure that the LLM is trained on diverse, high-quality data that accurately reflects the types of interactions the agent will encounter.

2. **Context Management**: Implement robust context management and memory mechanisms to track the conversation flow and preserve important details across multiple turns.
3. **Clarification Requests**: Program the LLM to ask clarifying questions when it encounters ambiguity in user inputs (e.g., "Could you please provide more details?").

Example: Handling Ambiguous Queries with Clarification

```
class LLMAgent:
    def __init__(self):
        self.context = {}

    def process_input(self, user_input):
        if "weather" in user_input:
            return "I can provide the weather. Could you
specify the location and date?"
        elif "flight" in user_input:
            return "I can help with flight bookings. Please
provide your destination and travel dates."
        else:
            return "I'm sorry, I didn't quite catch that. Can
you clarify your request?"

# Example usage
agent = LLMAgent()
response = agent.process_input("What's the weather?")
print(response)
```

-   Here, the agent asks for clarification when the user's query lacks necessary details, ensuring it provides the right response.

Issue 2: Performance Lag and Slow Response Time

Another common issue faced by LLM agents is slow response times, which can be caused by excessive computational load, inefficient algorithms, or resource limitations.

Potential Causes:

-   **Model Size**: Large LLMs may require significant computational resources for inference, causing delays in processing.
-   **Server Overload**: Insufficient server capacity or overloading of the system can lead to delays in processing requests.

- **Inefficient Code**: Poorly optimized code or algorithms that handle data inefficiently can contribute to slow performance.

Solutions:

1. **Model Optimization**: Use techniques like **model pruning**, **quantization**, and **distillation** to reduce the size of the model without sacrificing performance. This can help improve response times by decreasing the amount of computation required.
2. **Load Balancing**: Distribute the computational load across multiple servers or processes to prevent any single server from becoming overloaded.
3. **Caching**: Cache frequently requested responses to reduce the need for repeated computations.

Example: Model Pruning for Performance Improvement

```python
import torch
import torch.nn as nn

class SimpleModel(nn.Module):
    def __init__(self):
        super(SimpleModel, self).__init__()
        self.fc1 = nn.Linear(10, 10)
        self.fc2 = nn.Linear(10, 1)

    def forward(self, x):
        x = torch.relu(self.fc1(x))
        x = self.fc2(x)
        return x

# Prune the model (simplified example)
def prune_model(model):
    for name, module in model.named_modules():
        if isinstance(module, nn.Linear):
            torch.nn.utils.prune.l1_unstructured(module,
name='weight', amount=0.2)

model = SimpleModel()
prune_model(model)
print(model)
```

- This example shows a simple pruning technique to reduce the model size and improve performance by removing unimportant weights.

2. Monitoring and Diagnostics

Effective monitoring and diagnostics are essential for maintaining the health and performance of LLM agents. By tracking key performance indicators (KPIs) and diagnosing issues before they become critical, developers can ensure smooth operations and high-quality service.

Key Monitoring Metrics:

1. **Response Accuracy**: Measure the percentage of correct or relevant responses. This can be assessed by comparing the agent's responses to a set of known correct answers or using user feedback.
2. **System Latency**: Track how long the agent takes to respond to a user input. High latency may indicate performance bottlenecks that need attention.
3. **User Engagement**: Measure how long users interact with the system and how often they return. High engagement indicates that users find the agent valuable and easy to interact with.
4. **Error Rates**: Track the frequency of errors or failures in the system. This includes unhandled exceptions, misinterpretations of user input, or technical failures in the underlying infrastructure.

Monitoring Tools and Techniques:

1. **Log Analysis**: Use logging frameworks to record every interaction with the LLM agent. Logs provide valuable insights into errors, performance issues, and user behavior.
2. **Real-Time Dashboards**: Implement real-time dashboards to visualize metrics like response time, system load, and user engagement. This helps developers quickly spot and address performance issues.
3. **Error Tracking Tools**: Use error-tracking tools (e.g., Sentry, New Relic) to identify, log, and track the frequency of errors and exceptions in real time.

Example: Basic Logging for Diagnostics

```
import logging

# Configure logging
logging.basicConfig(filename='llm_agent.log',
level=logging.INFO)
```

```
class LLMAgent:
    def process_input(self, user_input):
        logging.info(f"Processing input: {user_input}")
        if "weather" in user_input:
            return "Here's the weather forecast for today."
        else:
            logging.error(f"Failed to understand input:
{user_input}")
            return "Sorry, I didn't catch that."

# Example usage
agent = LLMAgent()
print(agent.process_input("What's the weather?"))
print(agent.process_input("What's the capital of France?"))
```

- This example logs both user inputs and errors, providing a clear record for troubleshooting. Monitoring logs helps detect issues early and take corrective action.

---

3. Continuous Improvement Strategies

To ensure that LLM agents remain effective and meet evolving user needs, continuous improvement is vital. This includes refining the agent's performance, updating its knowledge base, and optimizing its algorithms. Developers should adopt strategies that focus on iterative enhancements based on user feedback, performance data, and new technological advancements.

Strategies for Continuous Improvement:

1. **Feedback Loops**:
   o Regularly collect and analyze user feedback to identify areas for improvement. This can include user ratings, surveys, and direct feedback from interactions.
   o Use this data to fine-tune the model's behavior, improve its response accuracy, and adapt its tone and personality to better match user expectations.
2. **Model Retraining**:
   o Periodically retrain the LLM on new, high-quality data to improve its accuracy and relevance. This is particularly important for keeping the agent up-to-date with current information and adapting to changing user needs.

o   Incorporate continuous learning techniques, such as **active learning**, to allow the model to learn from user interactions in real time.

3. **Performance Tuning**:
    o   Continuously monitor the performance of the LLM agent and optimize the system for faster responses, lower latency, and reduced computational costs.
    o   Implement more efficient algorithms, pruning, and compression techniques to improve the agent's performance over time.

4. **A/B Testing**:
    o   Use A/B testing to evaluate different versions of the LLM agent's responses, user interface, or functionality. This helps identify the most effective strategies and ensures the agent's continuous improvement based on actual user preferences.

Example: Simple Feedback Integration

```
class FeedbackSystem:
    def __init__(self):
        self.feedback = []

    def collect_feedback(self, user_rating, user_comment):
        self.feedback.append({'rating': user_rating,
'comment': user_comment})

    def analyze_feedback(self):
        positive_feedback = [f for f in self.feedback if
f['rating'] >= 4]
        return len(positive_feedback), len(self.feedback)

# Example usage
feedback_system = FeedbackSystem()
feedback_system.collect_feedback(5, "Excellent service!")
feedback_system.collect_feedback(3, "The response time was
slow.")
positive_feedback, total_feedback =
feedback_system.analyze_feedback()

print(f"Positive Feedback:
{positive_feedback}/{total_feedback} responses")
```

- In this example, a simple feedback system is implemented to collect and analyze user ratings. Positive feedback is tracked to help improve the agent's performance.

Troubleshooting and maintaining LLM agents require ongoing attention and proactive strategies. By identifying common issues, such as inaccurate responses and performance lag, and addressing them with clear solutions, developers can ensure that their agents continue to provide high-quality service. Regular monitoring and diagnostics are essential for spotting problems early and optimizing system performance. Finally, continuous improvement strategies—such as feedback loops, retraining, and performance tuning—ensure that the LLM agent evolves alongside user needs and technological advancements. By following these practices, developers can create reliable, efficient, and user-friendly LLM agents that remain effective in the long term.

Chapter 20: Troubleshooting and Maintaining LLM Agents

Building and deploying a Large Language Model (LLM) agent is a significant technical achievement, but its journey does not end once it is launched. Continuous maintenance and troubleshooting are essential to ensuring that the agent remains reliable, efficient, and effective in meeting users' needs. This chapter will cover the common issues that developers face with LLM agents, strategies for monitoring and diagnosing problems, and techniques for the continuous improvement of these systems.

1. Common Issues and Solutions

While LLM agents are designed to handle a wide range of tasks, they may experience issues related to accuracy, performance, and user experience. Addressing these issues promptly and effectively is key to maintaining a robust system.

Issue 1: Inaccurate or Irrelevant Responses

LLM agents may sometimes produce responses that are inaccurate, irrelevant, or incomplete. This issue can stem from several factors, including poor training data, a lack of contextual understanding, or the model's failure to interpret user intent properly.

Potential Causes:

- **Insufficient or Biased Training Data**: If the model was trained on unrepresentative or biased data, it may produce incorrect responses.
- **Context Loss**: In multi-turn conversations, LLM agents may lose track of the context, resulting in incoherent or irrelevant replies.
- **Ambiguity in User Queries**: If a user's query is vague or ambiguous, the model may misinterpret it and give an incorrect response.

Solutions:

1. **Improving Training Data**: Ensure that the LLM is trained on diverse, high-quality data that accurately reflects the types of interactions the agent will encounter.

2. **Context Management**: Implement robust context management and memory mechanisms to track the conversation flow and preserve important details across multiple turns.
3. **Clarification Requests**: Program the LLM to ask clarifying questions when it encounters ambiguity in user inputs (e.g., "Could you please provide more details?").

Example: Handling Ambiguous Queries with Clarification

```
class LLMAgent:
    def __init__(self):
        self.context = {}

    def process_input(self, user_input):
        if "weather" in user_input:
            return "I can provide the weather. Could you
specify the location and date?"
        elif "flight" in user_input:
            return "I can help with flight bookings. Please
provide your destination and travel dates."
        else:
            return "I'm sorry, I didn't quite catch that. Can
you clarify your request?"

# Example usage
agent = LLMAgent()
response = agent.process_input("What's the weather?")
print(response)
```

- Here, the agent asks for clarification when the user's query lacks necessary details, ensuring it provides the right response.

Issue 2: Performance Lag and Slow Response Time

Another common issue faced by LLM agents is slow response times, which can be caused by excessive computational load, inefficient algorithms, or resource limitations.

Potential Causes:

- **Model Size**: Large LLMs may require significant computational resources for inference, causing delays in processing.
- **Server Overload**: Insufficient server capacity or overloading of the system can lead to delays in processing requests.

- **Inefficient Code**: Poorly optimized code or algorithms that handle data inefficiently can contribute to slow performance.

Solutions:

1. **Model Optimization**: Use techniques like **model pruning, quantization**, and **distillation** to reduce the size of the model without sacrificing performance. This can help improve response times by decreasing the amount of computation required.
2. **Load Balancing**: Distribute the computational load across multiple servers or processes to prevent any single server from becoming overloaded.
3. **Caching**: Cache frequently requested responses to reduce the need for repeated computations.

Example: Model Pruning for Performance Improvement

```
import torch
import torch.nn as nn

class SimpleModel(nn.Module):
    def __init__(self):
        super(SimpleModel, self).__init__()
        self.fc1 = nn.Linear(10, 10)
        self.fc2 = nn.Linear(10, 1)

    def forward(self, x):
        x = torch.relu(self.fc1(x))
        x = self.fc2(x)
        return x

# Prune the model (simplified example)
def prune_model(model):
    for name, module in model.named_modules():
        if isinstance(module, nn.Linear):
            torch.nn.utils.prune.l1_unstructured(module,
name='weight', amount=0.2)

model = SimpleModel()
prune_model(model)
print(model)
```

- This example shows a simple pruning technique to reduce the model size and improve performance by removing unimportant weights.

2. Monitoring and Diagnostics

Effective monitoring and diagnostics are essential for maintaining the health and performance of LLM agents. By tracking key performance indicators (KPIs) and diagnosing issues before they become critical, developers can ensure smooth operations and high-quality service.

Key Monitoring Metrics:

1. **Response Accuracy**: Measure the percentage of correct or relevant responses. This can be assessed by comparing the agent's responses to a set of known correct answers or using user feedback.
2. **System Latency**: Track how long the agent takes to respond to a user input. High latency may indicate performance bottlenecks that need attention.
3. **User Engagement**: Measure how long users interact with the system and how often they return. High engagement indicates that users find the agent valuable and easy to interact with.
4. **Error Rates**: Track the frequency of errors or failures in the system. This includes unhandled exceptions, misinterpretations of user input, or technical failures in the underlying infrastructure.

Monitoring Tools and Techniques:

1. **Log Analysis**: Use logging frameworks to record every interaction with the LLM agent. Logs provide valuable insights into errors, performance issues, and user behavior.
2. **Real-Time Dashboards**: Implement real-time dashboards to visualize metrics like response time, system load, and user engagement. This helps developers quickly spot and address performance issues.
3. **Error Tracking Tools**: Use error-tracking tools (e.g., Sentry, New Relic) to identify, log, and track the frequency of errors and exceptions in real time.

Example: Basic Logging for Diagnostics

```
import logging

# Configure logging
logging.basicConfig(filename='llm_agent.log',
level=logging.INFO)
```

```
class LLMAgent:
    def process_input(self, user_input):
        logging.info(f"Processing input: {user_input}")
        if "weather" in user_input:
            return "Here's the weather forecast for today."
        else:
            logging.error(f"Failed to understand input:
{user_input}")
            return "Sorry, I didn't catch that."

# Example usage
agent = LLMAgent()
print(agent.process_input("What's the weather?"))
print(agent.process_input("What's the capital of France?"))
```

- This example logs both user inputs and errors, providing a clear record for troubleshooting. Monitoring logs helps detect issues early and take corrective action.

---

3. Continuous Improvement Strategies

To ensure that LLM agents remain effective and meet evolving user needs, continuous improvement is vital. This includes refining the agent's performance, updating its knowledge base, and optimizing its algorithms. Developers should adopt strategies that focus on iterative enhancements based on user feedback, performance data, and new technological advancements.

Strategies for Continuous Improvement:

1. **Feedback Loops**:
   - Regularly collect and analyze user feedback to identify areas for improvement. This can include user ratings, surveys, and direct feedback from interactions.
   - Use this data to fine-tune the model's behavior, improve its response accuracy, and adapt its tone and personality to better match user expectations.
2. **Model Retraining**:
   - Periodically retrain the LLM on new, high-quality data to improve its accuracy and relevance. This is particularly important for keeping the agent up-to-date with current information and adapting to changing user needs.

- o Incorporate continuous learning techniques, such as **active learning**, to allow the model to learn from user interactions in real time.
3. **Performance Tuning**:
   - o Continuously monitor the performance of the LLM agent and optimize the system for faster responses, lower latency, and reduced computational costs.
   - o Implement more efficient algorithms, pruning, and compression techniques to improve the agent's performance over time.
4. **A/B Testing**:
   - o Use A/B testing to evaluate different versions of the LLM agent's responses, user interface, or functionality. This helps identify the most effective strategies and ensures the agent's continuous improvement based on actual user preferences.

Example: Simple Feedback Integration

```python
class FeedbackSystem:
    def __init__(self):
        self.feedback = []

    def collect_feedback(self, user_rating, user_comment):
        self.feedback.append({'rating': user_rating,
'comment': user_comment})

    def analyze_feedback(self):
        positive_feedback = [f for f in self.feedback if
f['rating'] >= 4]
        return len(positive_feedback), len(self.feedback)

# Example usage
feedback_system = FeedbackSystem()
feedback_system.collect_feedback(5, "Excellent service!")
feedback_system.collect_feedback(3, "The response time was
slow.")
positive_feedback, total_feedback =
feedback_system.analyze_feedback()

print(f"Positive Feedback:
{positive_feedback}/{total_feedback} responses")
```

- In this example, a simple feedback system is implemented to collect and analyze user ratings. Positive feedback is tracked to help improve the agent's performance.

Troubleshooting and maintaining LLM agents require ongoing attention and proactive strategies. By identifying common issues, such as inaccurate responses and performance lag, and addressing them with clear solutions, developers can ensure that their agents continue to provide high-quality service. Regular monitoring and diagnostics are essential for spotting problems early and optimizing system performance. Finally, continuous improvement strategies—such as feedback loops, retraining, and performance tuning—ensure that the LLM agent evolves alongside user needs and technological advancements. By following these practices, developers can create reliable, efficient, and user-friendly LLM agents that remain effective in the long term.

Chapter 21: Collaborative Development of LLM Agents

The development of Large Language Models (LLMs) and their integration into real-world applications requires the combined expertise of professionals from diverse backgrounds. Collaborative development fosters innovation, improves efficiency, and ensures the creation of robust, scalable, and user-centric LLM agents. In this chapter, we will explore key principles for building effective AI teams, the tools and practices that facilitate collaboration, and the challenges and strategies for managing multi-disciplinary projects in the development of LLM agents.

1. Building Effective AI Teams

Building an effective AI team is crucial for the success of LLM agent development. AI projects, particularly those involving large-scale models like LLMs, require a diverse set of skills. The team should consist of individuals who bring complementary expertise, allowing for a holistic approach to development, testing, and deployment.

Key Roles in an AI Team:

1. **Data Scientists**:
   - **Responsibilities**: Data scientists are responsible for analyzing data, training the LLM, evaluating its performance, and fine-tuning the model. They use statistical analysis, machine learning algorithms, and domain-specific knowledge to improve the model's effectiveness.
   - **Skills**: Strong knowledge of machine learning, data manipulation, statistical analysis, and programming (typically in Python).
2. **Machine Learning Engineers**:
   - **Responsibilities**: Machine learning engineers focus on designing and building the systems and infrastructure needed to support the LLM agent. This includes training models at scale, optimizing performance, and managing deployment pipelines.
   - **Skills**: Proficiency in deep learning frameworks (e.g., TensorFlow, PyTorch), systems programming, and cloud computing.

3. **AI Research Scientists**:
   - o **Responsibilities**: These team members are responsible for advancing the theoretical foundations of LLMs. They focus on novel approaches to improving model architecture, algorithms, and training methods.
   - o **Skills**: Strong background in AI theory, research, and advanced mathematical concepts like neural networks, optimization, and natural language processing (NLP).
4. **UX/UI Designers**:
   - o **Responsibilities**: UX/UI designers ensure that the LLM agent provides a seamless, user-friendly experience. They focus on the interaction flow, visual design, and ensuring that the agent is intuitive and easy to use.
   - o **Skills**: Expertise in user interface design, prototyping, usability testing, and understanding user needs.
5. **DevOps Engineers**:
   - o **Responsibilities**: DevOps engineers manage the infrastructure, deployment, and maintenance of the LLM agent. They ensure the systems are scalable, reliable, and performant in production environments.
   - o **Skills**: Knowledge of cloud platforms (e.g., AWS, Azure), containerization (Docker, Kubernetes), and automation.
6. **Ethicists and Legal Advisors**:
   - o **Responsibilities**: Given the ethical and legal implications of LLM agents, ethicists and legal advisors play an important role in ensuring that the system adheres to ethical standards and complies with data privacy and security regulations.
   - o **Skills**: Expertise in ethics, law, and AI governance.

Building a Collaborative Team Culture

For a team to work effectively, collaboration and communication are key. Here are a few practices to foster a productive team environment:

- **Clear Communication**: Use platforms like Slack or Microsoft Teams for day-to-day communication. Regular meetings (e.g., stand-ups or sprint planning) ensure that everyone is on the same page.
- **Cross-Functional Collaboration**: Encourage collaboration between roles. For example, data scientists and UX/UI designers can work together to ensure that the LLM's responses are not only accurate but also user-friendly.

- **Diverse Perspectives**: Having a diverse team, with a mix of backgrounds, experiences, and skills, promotes innovation and helps identify potential issues from different viewpoints.

---

2. Collaboration Tools and Practices

Effective collaboration tools and practices are essential for managing the complexity of LLM agent development. These tools help coordinate workflows, facilitate communication, and track progress.

Collaboration Tools for AI Development:

1. **Version Control Systems (e.g., GitHub, GitLab):**
   - **Purpose**: Version control allows teams to collaboratively work on code, track changes, and merge contributions. GitHub and GitLab are popular platforms for managing source code, reviewing pull requests, and ensuring that team members can work concurrently without conflicts.
   - **Example**: Using GitHub to manage code for the LLM's underlying algorithms and infrastructure ensures that changes are tracked and versioned appropriately, making it easier to collaborate and roll back to previous versions if needed.
2. **Project Management Tools (e.g., Jira, Trello, Asana):**
   - **Purpose**: Project management tools help organize tasks, assign responsibilities, and track deadlines. These tools allow teams to break down complex projects into smaller tasks, prioritize them, and ensure that everything is on track.
   - **Example**: Jira is commonly used in agile development to manage sprints, track issues, and plan releases. It can also be used to assign tasks related to LLM training, testing, and deployment.
3. **Continuous Integration and Continuous Deployment (CI/CD) Tools (e.g., Jenkins, GitHub Actions, CircleCI):**
   - **Purpose**: CI/CD tools automate the process of integrating new code changes and deploying them to production. This helps maintain a fast-paced development cycle and ensures that new features or fixes are seamlessly integrated and deployed without issues.

- o **Example**: Using GitHub Actions to automatically train the LLM on new data and deploy updates ensures that the model stays up to date with minimal manual intervention.
4. **Collaborative Coding Environments (e.g., Google Colab, Jupyter Notebooks)**:
   - o **Purpose**: These platforms allow multiple team members to work on code and data analysis collaboratively, in real time, making it easier for data scientists and machine learning engineers to develop and test models together.
   - o **Example**: Google Colab is particularly useful for teams working on machine learning projects because it provides a shared environment where teams can access pre-configured hardware accelerators (GPUs/TPUs) for model training.
5. **Communication and Feedback Tools (e.g., Slack, Zoom, Miro)**:
   - o **Purpose**: These tools facilitate communication and allow teams to give and receive feedback quickly. Virtual meetings, brainstorming sessions, and design reviews are integral to keeping everyone aligned and moving forward.
   - o **Example**: Slack can be used for real-time communication, while Zoom meetings are great for discussing complex issues or conducting live reviews of the agent's performance.

Collaborative Practices for AI Development:

- **Agile Methodology**: Agile practices such as sprints, scrum meetings, and backlog grooming help break down the project into manageable tasks. This allows for iterative development and regular feedback, ensuring that the agent evolves according to the team's vision and user needs.
- **Code Reviews**: Peer reviews of code ensure that the codebase remains clean, maintainable, and free of errors. Code reviews are a collaborative process where team members provide feedback on each other's work, which improves quality and encourages knowledge sharing.
- **Pair Programming**: Pair programming is a technique where two developers work together at one workstation. One writes code while the other reviews it in real time. This practice can be highly effective in improving code quality and fostering collaboration.

Example: Using GitHub for Code Review

```
# Step-by-step process for code review on GitHub
```

```
1. Push the feature branch to the GitHub repository.
2. Create a pull request (PR) for your branch.
3. Assign a team member as a reviewer.
4. The reviewer comments, suggests improvements, or approves
the changes.
5. Merge the PR after it has been reviewed and approved.

# Commands for GitHub:
git checkout -b feature/new-llm-agent
git add .
git commit -m "Implement new feature for LLM agent"
git push origin feature/new-llm-agent
```

- In this process, code changes are reviewed through pull requests on GitHub, enabling easy collaboration between developers.

---

3. Managing Multi-Disciplinary Projects

LLM agent development often involves teams of experts from various disciplines, such as AI research, data science, machine learning, UX/UI design, ethics, and legal affairs. Managing multi-disciplinary projects can be challenging, but with the right approach, it can lead to the creation of highly effective and well-rounded LLM agents.

Challenges in Multi-Disciplinary Collaboration:

1. **Different Terminologies and Approaches**: Each discipline has its own set of terminology, methodologies, and goals, which can create confusion or misalignment. For example, an AI researcher may focus on optimizing the model's performance, while a UX designer may prioritize how users interact with the agent.
2. **Balancing Priorities**: Different teams may have competing priorities. For instance, machine learning engineers may prioritize model efficiency, while the UX team may focus on ensuring that the agent is easy and pleasant to use.
3. **Coordinating Timelines**: Different aspects of the project, such as training the LLM, designing the user interface, and ensuring legal compliance, may operate on different timelines. Coordinating these tasks and ensuring smooth integration is crucial.

Strategies for Managing Multi-Disciplinary Projects:

1. **Clear Communication**: Ensuring that all team members are aligned on the project's objectives and expectations is key to successful collaboration. Regular cross-disciplinary meetings where each team shares progress and insights can bridge gaps between disciplines.
2. **Defining Roles and Responsibilities**: Clearly outlining each team member's role and responsibilities prevents overlap and confusion. Each discipline's contributions should be valued and integrated into the overall project goals.
3. **Centralized Project Management**: Using project management tools like Jira or Asana to track progress, assign tasks, and monitor deadlines helps manage the complexities of multi-disciplinary projects. This ensures that all team members are aware of milestones, deadlines, and dependencies.
4. **Iterative Development**: As with agile methodology, iterative development allows different teams to contribute incrementally to the project. For example, the machine learning team can train the initial LLM model, while the UX team works on designing the user interface, and the legal team reviews compliance at each stage.

Example: Coordinating Multi-Disciplinary Work with Jira

```
# Example of Jira workflow for a multi-disciplinary LLM
project:
1. Create a project in Jira titled "LLM Agent Development".
2. Define Epics: "Model Training", "UX Design", "Legal
Review", "Testing".
3. Break each Epic into smaller tasks (e.g., "Train LLM on
new dataset", "Design UI for agent").
4. Assign tasks to relevant teams (Data Science, UX Design,
Legal).
5. Set deadlines and track progress via Jira boards.
6. Hold weekly stand-ups for all teams to discuss progress
and address blockers.
```

- Using Jira helps coordinate tasks, track progress, and ensure all teams are working together towards a unified goal.

Successful collaborative development of LLM agents requires diverse expertise, clear communication, and well-organized project management. By building effective AI teams with complementary skills, leveraging collaboration tools, and managing multi-disciplinary projects effectively, developers can ensure the creation of robust and user-centric LLM agents. Collaboration fosters innovation, accelerates problem-solving, and leads to the development of LLM agents that meet the evolving needs of users and industries.

Chapter 22: Implementing Ethical AI Practices

As the capabilities of AI systems, particularly Large Language Models (LLMs), continue to expand, it becomes increasingly important to ensure that these systems are developed and deployed ethically. The impact of AI technologies on society can be profound, ranging from their role in enhancing decision-making to their potential to perpetuate biases and inequalities. In this chapter, we will explore the importance of developing ethical guidelines for AI systems, review case studies that illustrate ethical AI implementation, and discuss how to balance innovation with responsibility.

1. Developing Ethical Guidelines

Ethical guidelines for AI are essential to ensure that AI systems operate in a way that aligns with societal values, protects human rights, and minimizes harm. Ethical AI practices provide a framework for developers, organizations, and policymakers to follow when designing, training, and deploying AI systems.

Key Principles of Ethical AI:

1. **Fairness**:
    o   **Definition**: Fairness in AI refers to ensuring that AI systems do not discriminate against individuals or groups based on sensitive attributes such as race, gender, age, or socio-economic status.
    o   **Implementation**: Fairness can be achieved by auditing datasets for bias, ensuring diverse representation in training data, and using fairness-aware algorithms. Continuous monitoring of AI outcomes is necessary to identify and mitigate any bias that may emerge.
    o   **Example**: An AI-powered hiring tool should be regularly checked to ensure it does not favor one gender over another or disadvantage certain ethnic groups.
2. **Transparency**:
    o   **Definition**: Transparency ensures that AI systems are explainable, so that users, stakeholders, and regulators can understand how decisions are made by the model.

- o **Implementation**: Developers should create clear documentation that explains how the model works, including the data it was trained on, the algorithms it uses, and how decisions are generated.
- o **Example**: An LLM that recommends legal advice should be able to explain the reasoning behind its recommendations, so that users can understand the basis for the suggestions.

3. **Accountability**:
   - o **Definition**: Accountability ensures that AI systems and their developers are responsible for the outcomes of AI-driven decisions.
   - o **Implementation**: Developers should document the decision-making process and establish clear lines of accountability in case an AI system causes harm. Legal frameworks and ethical guidelines should specify who is responsible for the actions of an AI system.
   - o **Example**: If an autonomous vehicle causes an accident, the company that developed the vehicle should be held accountable, and clear protocols should exist for handling such incidents.

4. **Privacy and Data Protection**:
   - o **Definition**: AI systems must respect user privacy and ensure that personal data is protected.
   - o **Implementation**: Developers must comply with privacy laws such as the General Data Protection Regulation (GDPR), use data anonymization techniques, and provide users with control over their personal information.
   - o **Example**: An AI health assistant must ensure that patient data is anonymized and securely stored, and it should give patients the option to opt-out or delete their data.

5. **Safety and Robustness**:
   - o **Definition**: AI systems should be designed to operate safely and handle unexpected situations without causing harm.
   - o **Implementation**: This can be achieved through rigorous testing, fail-safe mechanisms, and continuous monitoring to ensure that AI systems behave as expected in diverse real-world conditions.
   - o **Example**: A recommendation system should be tested for robustness to ensure it doesn't make unsafe or harmful suggestions, such as promoting harmful products or misinformation.

Developing Ethical Guidelines: To ensure the ethical use of LLMs and AI systems, organizations should adopt the following steps when developing their guidelines:

1. **Stakeholder Engagement**: Involve diverse stakeholders (e.g., ethicists, technologists, regulators, and affected communities) in the development of ethical guidelines.
2. **Documentation**: Develop clear and transparent documentation that outlines the ethical guidelines and how they will be enforced.
3. **Continuous Review**: Regularly review and update ethical guidelines to account for technological advancements, new societal concerns, and changing regulations.

---

2. Case Studies on Ethical AI Implementation

Implementing ethical AI practices requires real-world examples to show how these principles can be applied in practice. Below are several case studies that highlight the challenges and solutions related to ethical AI implementation.

Case Study 1: AI in Hiring – Addressing Bias in Recruitment Tools

A major technology company developed an AI-powered recruitment tool that was intended to streamline the hiring process. However, the system was found to be biased against female candidates, as it had been trained on historical hiring data that reflected gender biases.

Challenges:

- The training data was predominantly male, leading the AI to prefer male candidates.
- The system's decision-making process lacked transparency, making it difficult to identify the source of the bias.

Solutions:

- The company revised its data collection process to ensure that the training data was more representative and balanced across genders.
- Transparency was introduced by creating clear documentation about how the AI made decisions and what features were most influential.

- The AI system underwent regular audits for fairness and bias, and the company set up a review committee to oversee the ethical implications of its AI models.

Outcome:

- The company was able to improve the fairness of its recruitment tool and ensure that it did not perpetuate gender biases. The tool also became more transparent, giving candidates a better understanding of the hiring process.

Case Study 2: Healthcare – AI for Diagnosing Skin Cancer

A healthcare startup developed an AI system to assist doctors in diagnosing skin cancer from images. The AI system was trained using a large dataset of labeled images, but there were concerns about whether it would perform equitably across different skin tones.

Challenges:

- The dataset had limited diversity, with a disproportionate number of images from lighter-skinned patients.
- The system performed poorly when diagnosing patients with darker skin tones, potentially leading to misdiagnoses.

Solutions:

- The company sourced more diverse datasets, ensuring that the system was trained with a representative range of skin tones.
- Ethical guidelines were put in place to ensure that the AI system was tested for fairness before deployment.
- The model's performance was continuously monitored, and the system was updated periodically to ensure it remained accurate across all demographics.

Outcome:

- The AI system was successfully adapted to be more inclusive, improving diagnostic accuracy across all skin tones. The company also ensured that the system's development followed strict privacy and data protection regulations, including informed consent from patients.

Case Study 3: Autonomous Vehicles – Ethical Decision-Making in Crisis Scenarios

An autonomous vehicle company developed a self-driving car that had to make ethical decisions in life-threatening situations. The car's decision-making model was tested with scenarios where the vehicle had to decide between two harmful outcomes, such as swerving to avoid an obstacle and hitting a pedestrian or continuing straight and hitting another vehicle.

Challenges:

- The system faced ethical dilemmas regarding how to prioritize the lives of individuals.
- There were public concerns about the moral implications of programming such decisions into machines.

Solutions:

- The company consulted ethicists, legal experts, and the public to create a framework for ethical decision-making in crisis situations.
- The car's decision-making process was made transparent, and the public was informed of how the vehicle's algorithms worked to ensure the least harm.
- The vehicle was programmed to follow strict guidelines that prioritized human life while minimizing overall harm.

Outcome:

- The company implemented ethical decision-making protocols that gained public acceptance. The transparency of the process helped build trust with customers and regulators, while ensuring that the vehicle operated safely in complex environments.

---

3. Balancing Innovation with Responsibility

As AI continues to evolve, it is essential to balance innovation with ethical responsibility. The rapid pace of AI development often pushes boundaries, but this must be tempered with a clear focus on the societal impact and potential consequences.

Challenges in Balancing Innovation with Responsibility:

1. **Speed of Development vs. Ethical Considerations**:
   - In the race to develop cutting-edge technologies, there is often pressure to deploy solutions quickly without fully considering their ethical implications. This can lead to the creation of powerful technologies that are not adequately tested or vetted for bias, fairness, or safety.
2. **Profit Motives vs. Societal Good**:
   - Companies may prioritize profitability and market share over the long-term societal impact of their AI systems. For instance, an AI system that maximizes revenue for a company may unintentionally exploit vulnerable populations or perpetuate harmful behaviors.
3. **Global Inequalities**:
   - While AI offers solutions to problems in developed countries, there is a risk that these technologies could exacerbate existing inequalities in developing countries. Ensuring that AI benefits all of society and does not further widen the gap between the rich and poor is crucial.

Strategies for Balancing Innovation with Responsibility:

1. **Inclusive Design and Development**:
   - Involve diverse stakeholders in the design and development process to ensure that AI systems reflect a wide range of needs and perspectives. This includes engaging ethicists, social scientists, and affected communities in decision-making.
2. **Regulation and Governance**:
   - Governments and regulatory bodies should work together with companies to establish guidelines that ensure AI is developed responsibly. International cooperation is key to creating global standards for ethical AI.
3. **Ethical AI Frameworks**:
   - Organizations should adopt and implement ethical AI frameworks that balance innovation with the need for responsibility. This includes setting up oversight committees, ensuring transparency in AI development, and regularly auditing AI systems for compliance with ethical standards.

Example: Balancing Innovation with Responsibility

```
class EthicalAIModel:
    def __init__(self, innovation_level,
responsibility_level):
        self.innovation_level = innovation_level
        self.responsibility_level = responsibility_level

    def evaluate_balance(self):
        if self.innovation_level > self.responsibility_level:
            return "Warning: Innovation is outpacing ethical
considerations. Reassess the impact."
        elif self.innovation_level <
self.responsibility_level:
            return "Balanced: Ethical considerations are
prioritized alongside innovation."
        else:
            return "Perfect balance: Innovation and
responsibility are well-aligned."

# Example usage
model = EthicalAIModel(innovation_level=8,
responsibility_level=7)
print(model.evaluate_balance())
```

- This simple evaluation system checks whether the innovation in AI development is well-balanced with the ethical responsibility, guiding developers to align their goals.

Implementing ethical AI practices is essential for ensuring that AI technologies, such as LLM agents, are used in a way that benefits society while minimizing harm. Developing ethical guidelines based on fairness, transparency, accountability, and privacy is a critical first step. Case studies demonstrate how these principles can be successfully applied in real-world scenarios, from hiring systems to healthcare applications. Balancing innovation with responsibility is an ongoing challenge, but by engaging diverse stakeholders, adopting ethical frameworks, and ensuring transparency, we can navigate this balance and build AI systems that are both innovative and responsible. Ethical AI development is not just a technical requirement; it is a societal obligation.

Chapter 23: Monetizing LLM Agents

As Large Language Models (LLMs) continue to evolve, their potential to create value across various industries is immense. From providing customer service to enhancing business operations, LLM agents offer numerous opportunities for monetization. However, turning these agents into profitable ventures requires strategic business models, effective market analysis, and a clear approach to scaling and commercialization. This chapter explores various ways to monetize LLM agents, offers insights into identifying market opportunities, and discusses the steps to scale and commercialize AI solutions.

1. Business Models for AI Agents

The monetization of LLM agents can take several forms depending on the application, the value proposition, and the market needs. The key to a successful business model is aligning the AI solution with customer needs while ensuring that it can be effectively commercialized.

Key Business Models for AI Agents:

1. **Subscription-Based Model**:
    - **Overview**: In this model, customers pay a recurring fee for access to the LLM-powered service or platform. The subscription model works well for software-as-a-service (SaaS) applications that provide continuous updates and improvements.
    - **Example**: An LLM-powered virtual assistant for businesses that automates customer support could charge a monthly or yearly subscription fee based on the number of agents or interactions.

   Benefits:

    - Predictable revenue stream.
    - Recurring customer relationships.
    - Scalability as customer base grows.

   Example: Subscription Model Implementation

```
class SubscriptionService:
```

```python
def __init__(self, service_name, monthly_fee):
    self.service_name = service_name
    self.monthly_fee = monthly_fee
    self.customers = []

def add_customer(self, customer_name):
    self.customers.append(customer_name)
    return f"{customer_name} has been added to
{self.service_name} subscription."

def collect_payment(self):
    total_revenue = len(self.customers) *
self.monthly_fee
    return f"Total monthly revenue:
${total_revenue}"

# Example usage
service = SubscriptionService("AI Assistant", 50)
print(service.add_customer("Tech Corp"))
print(service.collect_payment())
```

- o In this example, a subscription model is implemented where a business can monetize an AI assistant by charging a fixed monthly fee per customer.
2. **Pay-Per-Use Model**:
   - o **Overview**: The pay-per-use model charges customers based on the amount of usage, such as the number of queries made to the AI agent or the number of hours the service is used.
   - o **Example**: A customer service chatbot powered by LLMs could charge businesses based on the volume of customer interactions handled by the bot.

Benefits:

- o Scalable pricing based on usage.
- o Flexibility for customers, as they only pay for what they use.

Example: Pay-Per-Use Model Implementation

```python
class PayPerUseService:
    def __init__(self, rate_per_query):
        self.rate_per_query = rate_per_query
        self.total_queries = 0

    def process_query(self):
        self.total_queries += 1
```

```
        return f"Processed query. Total queries:
{self.total_queries}"

    def calculate_payment(self):
        return f"Total amount due: ${self.total_queries
* self.rate_per_query}"

# Example usage
service = PayPerUseService(2)   # Charging $2 per query
print(service.process_query())
print(service.calculate_payment())
```

- o This example demonstrates how a pay-per-use model works by charging businesses based on the number of queries processed by the LLM agent.
3. **Freemium Model**:
   - o **Overview**: The freemium model offers basic services for free, while charging for premium features. This model is particularly effective for consumer-facing AI solutions, as it allows users to try the product before committing to a paid subscription.
   - o **Example**: An LLM-powered content generation tool could allow users to generate limited content for free, but charge for additional features like high-quality content, advanced customization, or unlimited usage.

Benefits:

- o Encourages user adoption and trial.
- o Potential to convert free users into paying customers through premium features.

Example: Freemium Model Implementation

```
class FreemiumService:
    def __init__(self, free_quota, premium_fee):
        self.free_quota = free_quota
        self.premium_fee = premium_fee
        self.usage_count = 0

    def use_service(self):
        if self.usage_count < self.free_quota:
            self.usage_count += 1
            return "Free usage within quota."
        else:
```

```
        return f"Upgrade to premium for
${self.premium_fee} to continue."

# Example usage
service = FreemiumService(5, 20)
print(service.use_service())
```

- o In this example, a freemium model is used where users can use the service for free up to a certain limit, after which they need to upgrade to a premium plan.

4. **Licensing Model**:
   - o **Overview**: Under the licensing model, businesses or other organizations pay for the right to use the LLM agent in their own products or services. This model is suitable for large-scale commercial applications or proprietary technologies.
   - o **Example**: A company could license its LLM-powered software to other businesses to be integrated into their own customer service platforms or business tools.

Benefits:

- o Potential for large one-time or recurring payments.
- o The ability to license the technology to multiple companies or industries.

Example: Licensing Model

```
class LicensingModel:
    def __init__(self, license_fee):
        self.license_fee = license_fee
        self.clients = []

    def license_software(self, client_name):
        self.clients.append(client_name)
        return f"{client_name} has licensed the
software for ${self.license_fee}."

# Example usage
licensing = LicensingModel(10000)   # One-time license
fee of $10,000
print(licensing.license_software("Global Corp"))
```

- o In this example, a licensing model is used where businesses can pay a fee to license the LLM software.

2. Market Analysis and Opportunity Identification

The success of an LLM agent depends not only on its technical capabilities but also on the ability to identify and capitalize on market opportunities. Market analysis helps determine where demand for LLM agents is greatest and identifies key factors that can influence adoption.

Key Steps for Market Analysis:

1. **Identifying Target Markets**:
   - **Vertical Markets**: LLM agents can be applied across various industries, including healthcare, finance, retail, education, and customer service. Identifying industries that would benefit most from automation, personalization, and efficiency gains is crucial.
   - **Use Case Focus**: Understanding the specific use cases in these industries is also important. For instance, in healthcare, LLM agents can assist with medical diagnoses or patient interaction, while in finance, they may be used for fraud detection or customer service.
2. **Assessing Market Demand**:
   - **Customer Needs**: Research the specific pain points that businesses or consumers face within each industry. Are there repetitive tasks that can be automated? Is there a need for better personalization?
   - **Market Size**: Estimate the size of the potential market. Larger markets, like customer service automation, may offer higher volume opportunities, but specialized markets, like legal AI assistants, may offer higher margins.
3. **Competitive Landscape**:
   - **Identifying Competitors**: Research existing competitors offering similar LLM solutions. Understanding their strengths and weaknesses can help position your product more effectively.
   - **Differentiation**: Identify how your LLM agent is different or better. Does it offer better performance, easier integration, more user-friendly interfaces, or lower cost?

Example: Identifying Market Opportunity

```
class MarketAnalysis:
    def __init__(self, industry, use_case,
competition_level):
        self.industry = industry
        self.use_case = use_case
        self.competition_level = competition_level

    def analyze_opportunity(self):
        if self.competition_level == "high":
            return f"The {self.industry} market is saturated.
Focus on differentiation."
        elif self.competition_level == "low":
            return f"The {self.industry} market has room for
growth. Opportunity exists."
        else:
            return f"The {self.industry} market is moderate.
Evaluate carefully."

# Example usage
analysis = MarketAnalysis("Healthcare", "Patient Support",
"low")
print(analysis.analyze_opportunity())
```

- This example simulates market analysis by assessing the competition level within a given industry and identifying opportunities for growth.

---

3. Scaling and Commercializing AI Solutions

Once a monetization strategy is in place and market opportunities are identified, the next step is scaling and commercializing the AI solution. This involves building a scalable infrastructure, marketing the solution effectively, and ensuring sustainable growth.

Key Strategies for Scaling and Commercializing AI Solutions:

1. **Infrastructure and Cloud Services**:
   - **Cloud Platforms**: Use cloud-based platforms like AWS, Google Cloud, or Microsoft Azure to scale AI solutions. These platforms offer flexible compute resources (e.g., GPUs) to handle large datasets and intensive computations required for LLM agents.

- o **Scalability**: Ensure that the AI solution can handle growing customer demands by implementing scalable architectures, such as containerized services and microservices.
2. **Marketing and Customer Acquisition**:
   - o **Targeted Marketing**: Focus on educating potential customers about the benefits of LLM agents in their specific industry. Demonstrating value through case studies, testimonials, and product demonstrations can help in customer acquisition.
   - o **Sales Channels**: Leverage various sales channels, including direct sales, resellers, and partnerships with other tech firms to expand the reach of the solution.
3. **Customer Support and Retention**:
   - o **Ongoing Support**: Provide excellent customer support to ensure that clients can effectively use and derive value from the AI solution. Regular updates, training, and troubleshooting will help retain customers.
   - o **Subscription and Upsell Opportunities**: Build long-term relationships by offering additional services, such as premium features, training packages, or customizations.

Example: Scaling AI Solutions with Cloud Infrastructure

```python
class CloudInfrastructure:
    def __init__(self, platform, scaling_method):
        self.platform = platform
        self.scaling_method = scaling_method

    def scale_solution(self):
        return f"Scaling AI solution using {self.platform}
with {self.scaling_method} method."

# Example usage
infrastructure = CloudInfrastructure("AWS", "auto-scaling")
print(infrastructure.scale_solution())
```

- • This example demonstrates how to scale AI solutions using cloud infrastructure, focusing on auto-scaling to handle increased demand.

Monetizing LLM agents requires strategic planning and understanding of the market, including identifying appropriate business models, analyzing opportunities, and scaling solutions effectively. Whether through subscription models, pay-per-use models, or licensing, there are multiple avenues for generating revenue from AI solutions. By assessing market demand, understanding the competitive landscape, and implementing scalable infrastructure, businesses can ensure the commercial success and sustainability of their AI products. Balancing innovation with ethical responsibility and providing ongoing customer support will further enhance the long-term success of LLM agents in the marketplace.

Conclusion

As we conclude this comprehensive guide on Large Language Model (LLM) agents, it's important to take a step back and reflect on the key concepts and insights we've discussed throughout the book. This conclusion will offer a recap of the major points, thoughts on the future of LLM agents, recommendations for continued learning and development, and a call to encourage innovation while maintaining ethical practices in the development of AI systems.

1. Recap of Key Concepts and Learnings

Throughout this book, we've delved into a range of topics related to the development, application, and monetization of LLM agents. Let's recap the major concepts and takeaways:

Introduction to LLM Agents

We began by defining what LLM agents are and how they differ from traditional AI agents. These systems are built upon advanced natural language processing techniques and are capable of understanding and generating human-like responses. LLMs have applications across a wide array of industries, such as healthcare, finance, education, and customer service.

Building and Designing LLM Agents

We covered the importance of designing effective LLM agents, including how to define objectives, map use cases, and select appropriate tools and frameworks. System architecture design, scalability, and flexibility were emphasized as crucial components of successful agent deployment.

Training and Implementing LLM Agents

Training an LLM involves not only curating high-quality data but also addressing challenges such as bias, computational requirements, and performance optimization. We discussed the importance of efficient coding practices, the integration of core functionalities, and testing strategies to ensure robustness.

Ethics and Accountability

Ethics in AI development cannot be overstated. We examined key principles such as fairness, transparency, accountability, and privacy. Ethical AI practices, as well as regulatory frameworks, were explored to guide the responsible development of LLM agents. The role of AI in influencing society and ensuring legal compliance was also thoroughly addressed.

Monetization and Commercialization

We explored various business models that can be used to monetize LLM agents, including subscription, pay-per-use, and licensing models. The importance of market analysis, identifying opportunities, and scaling solutions was discussed as a key factor in successful commercialization.

Collaboration and Teamwork

Building LLM agents requires interdisciplinary collaboration. We emphasized the need for cross-functional teams with expertise in AI research, data science, machine learning, UX/UI design, and ethical considerations. Collaborative tools and project management practices ensure that teams can work efficiently and achieve shared goals.

Troubleshooting, Maintenance, and Continuous Improvement

We highlighted the importance of ongoing monitoring, diagnostics, and troubleshooting to maintain the health of LLM systems. Continuous improvement strategies, such as feedback loops, retraining, and performance tuning, are critical for adapting to evolving user needs and technological advancements.

---

2. Final Thoughts on the Future of LLM Agents

The future of LLM agents holds great promise, both in terms of technological innovation and their societal impact. As AI technology continues to advance, we can expect LLMs to become even more sophisticated, capable of performing increasingly complex tasks and offering even greater personalization. Key developments to watch for include:

- **Increased Autonomy and Intelligence**: LLM agents will become more autonomous, requiring less manual intervention and becoming capable of self-improvement through continuous learning and adaptation.

- **Cross-Modal Capabilities**: Future LLMs may integrate more seamlessly with other modalities beyond text, such as images, audio, and video, creating richer, more interactive experiences.
- **Ethical AI and Regulation**: As AI becomes more integrated into society, the development of regulatory frameworks and standards for ethical AI will be crucial. This will ensure that LLM agents continue to serve humanity while avoiding negative societal impacts.
- **Human-AI Collaboration**: Rather than replacing humans, LLM agents will increasingly complement human intelligence. These systems will work alongside humans in various roles, from healthcare to creative industries, improving productivity and decision-making.

Emerging Trends to Watch:

- **Personalized AI Experiences**: With advancements in personalization, LLMs will be able to understand and adapt to individual preferences more deeply, offering highly tailored recommendations, responses, and services.
- **Distributed and Decentralized AI**: Decentralized models may emerge, where AI agents are distributed across multiple nodes, creating more resilient, transparent, and efficient systems that operate on a larger scale.

As LLM agents become more advanced, their integration into various aspects of society will likely grow, creating transformative changes in business, governance, education, healthcare, and beyond.

---

3. Recommendations for Continued Learning and Development

To stay ahead in the rapidly evolving field of LLM agents and AI in general, it's essential to keep learning and adapting. Here are some recommendations for continued learning and development:

1. **Stay Updated on AI Research**:
   - AI is a constantly evolving field. Stay informed about the latest advancements in LLM research by reading academic papers, attending conferences, and following key researchers in the field.

- Key areas to focus on include advances in transformer models, self-supervised learning, multi-modal learning, and ethical AI development.
2. **Explore Open-Source Projects**:
   - Many cutting-edge LLM models are open source (e.g., OpenAI's GPT, Google's BERT). Contributing to these projects, or experimenting with them in your own work, is a great way to learn from the community and stay at the forefront of LLM technology.
3. **Enhance Your Skillset in Data Science and Machine Learning**:
   - To effectively build and fine-tune LLM agents, it is crucial to have a strong foundation in machine learning, natural language processing, and data science. Platforms like Coursera, edX, and fast.ai offer excellent resources for further education in these areas.
4. **Participate in AI Ethics Discussions**:
   - As ethical issues in AI become more prominent, it's important to engage in conversations about the societal impact of AI. Participating in discussions about AI ethics, regulations, and fairness will help shape the future of AI technology and ensure it benefits everyone.
5. **Experiment with Different LLM Use Cases**:
   - Gain hands-on experience by experimenting with LLMs in various real-world applications. Whether it's building chatbots, virtual assistants, content generators, or more complex AI systems, practical experience will enhance your understanding of the challenges and opportunities in this field.

---

4. Encouraging Innovation and Ethical Practices

The future of LLM agents is bright, but it is essential that innovation goes hand-in-hand with responsibility. As developers, researchers, and entrepreneurs, we must prioritize ethical considerations alongside technical innovation. By adhering to ethical guidelines, conducting thorough impact assessments, and creating systems that are fair, transparent, and accountable, we can ensure that LLM agents contribute positively to society.

Encouraging Responsible Innovation:

- **Inclusive Design**: Involve diverse voices from different communities, backgrounds, and disciplines when developing LLM agents. This will help ensure that AI solutions are inclusive and avoid biases that can arise from homogenous design teams.
- **Impact Assessments**: Regularly assess the impact of AI systems on users and society. Consider conducting ethical audits and gathering feedback from stakeholders to ensure the system's behavior aligns with societal values.
- **Commitment to Transparency**: Maintain transparency in both development and deployment. Clearly communicate the capabilities and limitations of your LLM agent, and allow users to understand how decisions are made by the system.
- **Collaboration Across Sectors**: Collaborate with policymakers, ethicists, and other stakeholders to ensure that AI technologies align with human-centric goals and remain accountable to societal needs.

Fostering Ethical AI Development:

Innovation is vital, but it must always be tempered with ethical responsibility. By embedding ethical principles into the development of LLM agents and prioritizing societal well-being, we can ensure that these technologies serve humanity in positive and meaningful ways.

The journey of building and deploying LLM agents is not just about technological achievement but also about fostering a future where AI serves as a positive force in society. This book has provided a comprehensive guide to LLM agents, from their technical foundations and design principles to ethical considerations and business strategies. As AI technology continues to advance, it is crucial that developers, businesses, and policymakers work together to harness its potential responsibly.

By embracing innovation, adhering to ethical practices, and prioritizing continuous learning, we can ensure that LLM agents and AI technologies contribute to creating a more intelligent, efficient, and equitable future for all.

Appendices

The appendices serve as a valuable resource for anyone seeking to deepen their understanding of Large Language Model (LLM) agents, offering additional resources, definitions, code examples, and step-by-step guides for practical implementation. Whether you are a beginner or an experienced developer, these appendices will provide you with essential tools and insights to further your knowledge and help you successfully build and deploy LLM agents.

---

1. Glossary of Terms

Understanding the terminology surrounding LLM agents and AI in general is crucial to effectively working with these technologies. Below is a comprehensive glossary of key terms and concepts.

Key Terms and Concepts:

- **Artificial Intelligence (AI)**: A branch of computer science that focuses on building machines capable of performing tasks that would normally require human intelligence, such as problem-solving, decision-making, language understanding, and learning.
- **Large Language Model (LLM)**: A type of AI model designed to process and generate human language. LLMs are typically built using deep learning techniques, particularly transformer networks, and are trained on vast amounts of textual data to understand, generate, and manipulate language.
- **Transformer Architecture**: A type of deep learning architecture used to model sequential data, particularly language. The transformer is designed to handle dependencies in data sequences and is the foundation of most state-of-the-art LLMs like GPT (Generative Pretrained Transformer) and BERT (Bidirectional Encoder Representations from Transformers).
- **Natural Language Processing (NLP)**: A field of AI that focuses on the interaction between computers and human language. NLP includes tasks such as language understanding, sentiment analysis, text generation, and machine translation.

- **Tokenization**: The process of breaking down text into smaller pieces (tokens), such as words or sub-words, to make it more manageable for models to process.
- **Training Data**: A large corpus of text data used to train machine learning models. For LLMs, this data is often collected from diverse sources, such as books, websites, and academic papers.
- **Fine-Tuning**: The process of taking a pre-trained model (such as an LLM) and training it further on a specific dataset to adapt it to a particular task or domain.
- **Bias in AI**: The tendency of AI models to make unfair or prejudiced decisions based on biases present in the training data. This can lead to negative societal impacts if not addressed during model development.
- **Explainability**: The ability of an AI system to explain its decision-making process in a manner understandable to humans. In LLMs, this often refers to techniques that allow users to understand how a model generated a particular response.
- **Reinforcement Learning**: A type of machine learning where an agent learns by interacting with its environment and receiving feedback in the form of rewards or penalties. This is commonly used for decision-making tasks.

---

2. Code Snippets and Templates

Below are several ready-to-use code examples and template architectures for building LLM agents. These examples cover some fundamental tasks in the development of LLM-based systems.

Code Snippets for Building LLM Agents:

Simple LLM Query Processor: This Python code demonstrates how to use a pre-trained transformer model for text generation using the `transformers` library.

```
from transformers import pipeline

# Load pre-trained model for text generation
generator = pipeline('text-generation', model='gpt-2')

# Function to generate text from input prompt
def generate_text(prompt, max_length=50):
```

```
    return generator(prompt, max_length=max_length,
num_return_sequences=1)

# Example usage
prompt = "Artificial Intelligence is revolutionizing"
generated_text = generate_text(prompt)
print(generated_text)
```

Explanation:

This code uses the `transformers` library to load the pre-trained
GPT-2 model for text generation.

The `generate_text` function generates a continuation of the
input prompt based on the model's understanding of language.

Tokenization with BERT: Tokenization is a critical step in NLP tasks.
This snippet demonstrates how to tokenize input text using a BERT
tokenizer.

```
from transformers import BertTokenizer

# Load pre-trained BERT tokenizer
tokenizer = BertTokenizer.from_pretrained('bert-base-
uncased')

# Function to tokenize input text
def tokenize_text(text):
    return tokenizer.tokenize(text)

# Example usage
text = "Natural Language Processing is fascinating."
tokens = tokenize_text(text)
print(tokens)
```

Explanation:

- This code snippet uses the BERT tokenizer from the
  `transformers` library to split the input text into tokens.
- Tokenization is essential for preparing the text to be
  processed by transformer models.

Template Architectures for LLM Agents:

1. **Basic LLM Agent Architecture**: The architecture of a basic LLM agent can be broken down into several stages: input processing, model inference, and output generation.

   Architecture Overview:

   - **Input Processing**: The input text is received from the user, tokenized, and preprocessed.
   - **Model Inference**: A pre-trained LLM is used to generate a response based on the input.
   - **Output Generation**: The generated output is post-processed and returned to the user.

   Template:

   ```
   +-----------------+                +-------------------+
   +----------------+
   | Input Processing |   ---->      | Model Inference   |
   ---->    | Output Generation|
   +-----------------+                +-------------------+
   +----------------+
   ```

   Explanation:

   - The agent takes in text, processes it through the LLM model, and then generates a response that is returned to the user.

2. **LLM with Memory for Conversational Agents**: A more advanced architecture includes a memory component to allow the LLM agent to remember past interactions, improving the continuity of conversations.

   Architecture Overview:

   - **Memory Module**: Stores previous user inputs and the agent's responses.
   - **Contextual Processing**: Retrieves the memory to inform the model's current response.
   - **Model Inference**: Uses the context provided by the memory module to generate more relevant responses.

Template:

```
+------------------+         +------------------------+
+--------------------+
| Memory Module    |  <-->   | Contextual Processing  |
--> | Model Inference   |
+------------------+         +------------------------+
+--------------------+
```

Explanation:

- o   This architecture is useful for building conversational agents
  that need to maintain context over multiple turns of dialogue.

---

3. Additional Resources and Further Reading

As the field of AI and LLM agents continues to grow, ongoing learning and
exploration are essential for staying ahead. Below is a curated list of
additional resources for further reading and study.

Recommended Books:

1. **"Deep Learning with Python" by François Chollet**: A highly
   accessible introduction to deep learning, covering both the theory and
   practical implementation of machine learning models, including
   neural networks.
2. **"Speech and Language Processing" by Daniel Jurafsky and
   James H. Martin**: A comprehensive textbook on natural language
   processing and computational linguistics, which serves as a valuable
   reference for anyone working with LLMs.
3. **"Transformers for Natural Language Processing" by Denis
   Rothman**: This book provides a detailed exploration of transformer
   models, their architectures, and their applications in NLP.

Research Papers:

1. **"Attention is All You Need" by Vaswani et al.**: The foundational
   paper introducing the transformer model, which is the backbone of
   many modern LLMs.
2. **"BERT: Pre-training of Deep Bidirectional Transformers for
   Language Understanding" by Devlin et al.**: This paper introduces

BERT, a transformer-based model that has set new records in NLP tasks.

Online Courses and Tutorials:

1. **Coursera: "Deep Learning Specialization" by Andrew Ng**: This series of courses provides a thorough introduction to deep learning, covering key concepts like neural networks and natural language processing.
2. **fast.ai: Practical Deep Learning for Coders**: A free course that teaches deep learning through hands-on projects using the fastai library.
3. **Hugging Face's Course on Transformers**: A free course dedicated to transformers and their use in NLP tasks, with practical tutorials using the Hugging Face library.

---

4. Setup Guides

Setting up a development environment for LLM agent development is essential for efficiently building, testing, and deploying these models. Below are step-by-step instructions for setting up key tools and libraries.

Step-by-Step Instructions for Setting Up Development Environments:

1. **Setting Up Python**:
    - o Install Python from the official Python website.
    - o Install pip (Python package installer) using the following command:
    - o `python -m ensurepip --upgrade`
2. **Installing TensorFlow and PyTorch**:
    - o TensorFlow and PyTorch are two of the most commonly used frameworks for training and deploying LLMs. To install TensorFlow:
    - o `pip install tensorflow`

    To install PyTorch:

    `pip install torch torchvision torchaudio`

3. **Installing the Hugging Face Transformers Library**: Hugging Face provides a popular library for working with pre-trained LLMs like GPT, BERT, and others.
4. ```
pip install transformers
```
5. **Setting Up Jupyter Notebooks**: Jupyter Notebooks are widely used for experimenting with machine learning models. Install Jupyter:
6. ```
pip install notebook
```

Launch Jupyter Notebook:

```
jupyter notebook
```

Installing and Configuring Necessary Tools and Libraries:

1. **CUDA for GPU Acceleration**: To take advantage of GPU acceleration, install the appropriate CUDA version for your hardware. For TensorFlow, install the GPU-enabled version:
2. ```
pip install tensorflow-gpu
```
3. **Set Up Version Control (Git)**: Install Git from Git's official site, and clone repositories to manage version control for your codebase:
4. ```
git clone https://github.com/your-repository.git
```

The appendices provide a robust toolkit for building, deploying, and scaling LLM agents. With a thorough understanding of the key terms, access to practical code examples, and the resources for further learning, you are well-equipped to dive deeper into the development of LLM-based applications. The setup guides ensure that you have the necessary tools and environments to start building and experimenting with your own AI solutions, while the recommended readings and courses will help you stay current with advancements in the field.

References

In this section, we provide a comprehensive list of the sources cited throughout the book. These resources include key books, academic journals, conferences, and online platforms that can help deepen your understanding of Large Language Models (LLMs), AI agents, and the various technologies discussed. Each reference is carefully selected to offer both foundational knowledge and cutting-edge research in the field of artificial intelligence, machine learning, and natural language processing (NLP).

Books

1. **Chollet, François. "Deep Learning with Python." Manning Publications, 2017.**
    - This book offers a hands-on introduction to deep learning using Python and Keras, providing insights into neural networks and their applications. It's particularly useful for understanding the core concepts behind many LLMs.
    - **Key Concepts**: Deep learning, neural networks, Keras, model training.
2. **Jurafsky, Daniel, and James H. Martin. "Speech and Language Processing." Prentice Hall, 2020.**
    - A comprehensive textbook on natural language processing and computational linguistics, this book covers everything from basic text processing techniques to advanced machine learning models, including LLMs.
    - **Key Concepts**: NLP, machine learning, speech processing, text analysis, sentiment analysis.
3. **Rothman, Denis. "Transformers for Natural Language Processing." Packt Publishing, 2021.**
    - This book provides a thorough examination of transformer architectures and their application in NLP tasks. It is particularly valuable for those interested in understanding the architecture of popular LLMs like GPT and BERT.
    - **Key Concepts**: Transformers, BERT, GPT, attention mechanisms, NLP applications.
4. **Devlin, Jacob, et al. "BERT: Pre-training of Deep Bidirectional Transformers for Language Understanding." arXiv, 2018.**
    - This paper introduces BERT (Bidirectional Encoder Representations from Transformers), one of the most influential models in the NLP space. It explains the

innovations that allowed BERT to achieve state-of-the-art results across several NLP tasks.
- o **Key Concepts**: BERT, transformers, pre-training, NLP benchmarks.

Journals and Research Papers

1. **Vaswani, Ashish, et al. "Attention is All You Need." Advances in Neural Information Processing Systems (NeurIPS), 2017.**
   - o The paper introduces the transformer architecture, a groundbreaking model for sequence-to-sequence tasks like translation, which laid the foundation for modern LLMs.
   - o **Key Concepts**: Transformers, self-attention, sequence-to-sequence tasks, neural networks.
2. **Radford, Alec, et al. "Improving Language Understanding by Generative Pre-Training." OpenAI, 2018.**
   - o This paper outlines the GPT model (Generative Pre-Training), which became a precursor to large-scale language models like GPT-3. The paper explores the importance of unsupervised learning in achieving high-quality language understanding.
   - o **Key Concepts**: GPT, generative pre-training, unsupervised learning, language understanding.
3. **Brown, Tom B., et al. "Language Models are Few-Shot Learners." arXiv, 2020.**
   - o This paper discusses GPT-3, one of the largest LLMs to date, and how it demonstrates the ability to perform tasks with minimal task-specific training (few-shot learning).
   - o **Key Concepts**: GPT-3, few-shot learning, language models, task adaptation.
4. **Bender, Emily M., et al. "On the Dangers of Stochastic Parrots: Can Language Models Be Too Big?" Proceedings of the 2021 ACM Conference on Fairness, Accountability, and Transparency (FAccT), 2021.**
   - o This paper critically evaluates the ethical implications of large language models, including concerns about their environmental impact, biases, and potential harm.
   - o **Key Concepts**: Ethical AI, LLMs, bias in AI, fairness, environmental impact.

Conferences and Workshops

1. **NeurIPS (Conference on Neural Information Processing Systems)**:
   - NeurIPS is one of the premier conferences in machine learning and AI. It covers all areas of AI research, including natural language processing, reinforcement learning, deep learning, and ethical AI.
   - **Key Topics**: Machine learning, AI research, deep learning, NLP, ethics in AI.
2. **ICML (International Conference on Machine Learning)**:
   - ICML is another leading conference where cutting-edge machine learning research, including work on LLMs, is presented. Papers from ICML often provide valuable insights into the latest advancements in deep learning and NLP techniques.
   - **Key Topics**: Machine learning models, AI research, model training, evaluation techniques.
3. **ACL (Association for Computational Linguistics Conference)**:
   - ACL is the top conference in the field of computational linguistics. It covers a wide range of topics related to NLP and language models, with a focus on advancing our understanding of how to build better language processing systems.
   - **Key Topics**: NLP, syntactic parsing, semantic understanding, language modeling, corpus-based studies.
4. **CVPR (Conference on Computer Vision and Pattern Recognition)**:
   - While primarily focused on computer vision, CVPR also features important research on multimodal AI, where LLMs are integrated with other modalities such as images and video.
   - **Key Topics**: Multimodal learning, computer vision, deep learning, LLMs, AI integration.

Online Resources

1. **Hugging Face**:
   - Hugging Face is a leading platform for NLP models, providing a comprehensive library (Transformers) that includes state-of-the-art LLMs like BERT, GPT, and T5. Their online documentation and tutorials are invaluable for anyone building or deploying LLMs.

- o **Website**: https://huggingface.co
- o **Key Features**: Pre-trained models, tutorials, community support, research papers, model deployment.
2. **Kaggle**:
    - o Kaggle is a platform for data science and machine learning competitions, but it also offers numerous datasets and tutorials related to NLP and LLMs. It's a great resource for hands-on practice with machine learning models.
    - o **Website**: https://www.kaggle.com
    - o **Key Features**: Datasets, notebooks, tutorials, competitions, machine learning challenges.
3. **Google AI Blog**:
    - o The Google AI Blog provides updates on the latest AI research, including breakthroughs in natural language processing and the development of LLMs. It's a great resource for staying informed about innovations in AI.
    - o **Website**: https://ai.googleblog.com
    - o **Key Topics**: LLM advancements, machine learning, AI research, Google AI projects.
4. **OpenAI Blog**:
    - o OpenAI's blog is an essential resource for anyone working with GPT and related models. It features research updates, tutorials, and discussions on the ethical implications of LLMs.
    - o **Website**: https://openai.com/blog
    - o **Key Topics**: GPT-3, LLMs, AI ethics, AI applications, research breakthroughs.

Further Reading

1. **"Artificial Intelligence: A Modern Approach" by Stuart Russell and Peter Norvig (Pearson, 2020)**:
    - o A comprehensive textbook that covers foundational concepts in artificial intelligence, including machine learning, problem-solving, and knowledge representation. This book is a great resource for those who want a broad understanding of AI.
2. **"Deep Reinforcement Learning Hands-On" by Maxim Lapan (Packt Publishing, 2018)**:
    - o This book provides practical insights into deep reinforcement learning, a branch of machine learning that can be combined with LLMs for decision-making tasks.

3. **"Machine Learning Yearning" by Andrew Ng**:
   - Although not a technical book, Andrew Ng's book offers a strategic guide to machine learning projects, helping developers make important decisions about model design, data, and infrastructure.
4. **"AI Ethics" by Mark Coeckelbergh (MIT Press, 2020)**:
   - A key resource for understanding the ethical issues in AI development. This book tackles issues such as fairness, transparency, accountability, and bias, which are crucial for responsible LLM development.

This references section provides an in-depth collection of essential readings, research papers, online resources, and tools for those interested in further exploring LLM agents, machine learning, and AI in general. By leveraging these resources, you can continue to expand your knowledge, stay up-to-date with the latest advancements, and apply these insights to your own AI projects. Whether you are just starting out or are an experienced developer, these references will support your ongoing learning journey in the rapidly evolving world of AI.

Index

The following index is designed to provide an alphabetical listing of the key topics, terms, concepts, and names mentioned throughout the book. It serves as a quick reference tool to help you easily locate specific sections, enabling you to navigate the content more efficiently and revisit important concepts as needed.

A

This index provides a thorough guide to quickly locate and revisit key topics and concepts discussed in this book. By organizing the subjects alphabetically, this index ensures that you can efficiently find relevant sections for deeper exploration. Whether you're interested in understanding technical details about LLMs, ethical considerations, business models, or implementation practices, the index serves as a valuable reference for both beginners and advanced users working with Large Language Model agents.

Companion Website

In today's fast-paced world, the need for immediate access to supplementary resources is crucial to enhancing your learning experience. The companion website for this book offers a wealth of additional materials, community support, and continuous updates to ensure that you can apply the knowledge gained effectively. Whether you are a developer looking for code examples, a student needing additional reading materials, or a professional seeking to discuss ideas with peers, the companion website serves as a central hub for all your needs.

1. Access to Supplementary Materials

The companion website provides access to essential supplementary resources that will help you dive deeper into the concepts discussed in this book. These resources include code repositories, downloadable resources such as templates and PDFs, and additional learning materials that will enhance your understanding and application of LLM agents.

Code Repositories (GitHub, GitLab Links)

The companion website offers direct links to public code repositories where you can find the source code examples used in the book. These repositories are hosted on popular platforms like GitHub and GitLab, ensuring that you have access to the latest versions of the code. You can explore, modify, and even contribute to the development of LLM agents by interacting with the code provided.

- **GitHub Repository**: The book's GitHub repository hosts all the code examples covered throughout the chapters. You can clone or download the repository, check for updates, and track changes as new versions of the book are released.
  - **Key Features**:
    - Full implementation of LLM agent examples.
    - Code for setting up the development environment.
    - Integration examples with external services and APIs.
    - Real-world case studies and additional examples.

    Example of using GitHub to access the repository:

    ```
    git clone
    https://github.com/yourusername/LLMAgents.git
    cd LLMAgents
    ```

- **GitLab Repository**: Similar to GitHub, the GitLab repository provides a collaborative platform where users can access the project, fork it, and make contributions. GitLab can be especially useful for teams working on larger projects and for integrating DevOps practices.
  - **Key Features**:
    - Continuous integration and deployment pipelines (CI/CD).
    - Documentation for setting up and running the models.
    - Collaborative tools for peer review and code sharing.

Downloadable Resources (PDFs, Templates)

The companion website also hosts downloadable resources that can complement the learning experience. These resources include PDFs for offline reading, templates for setting up your own LLM agent frameworks, and additional documentation to guide you through more advanced topics.

- **PDF Versions of the Book**: You can download the entire book or specific chapters in PDF format for offline access. This allows you to read and reference the content on any device, even without an internet connection.
- **Template Architectures**: For those interested in applying what they've learned, templates for various architectures (e.g., LLM with memory, chatbots, etc.) are available. These templates will help you get started quickly by providing a solid foundation upon which to build and customize your LLM agents.

  Example of using templates:

    - **Basic LLM Chatbot Template**: This template can be used to create a conversational agent, which you can modify to meet specific business needs.
    - **Memory-Based LLM Architecture Template**: This template allows you to build a conversational agent that retains context over multiple interactions.

Example of Download Link:

- **Access the PDF version of the book**: Download PDF
- **Download Templates**: Access Templates

---

2. Community and Support

The companion website is not just a repository for code and materials but also serves as a vibrant hub for community interaction and support. Here, you can engage with other learners, developers, and experts to discuss ideas, share experiences, and get help with challenges you may encounter.

Forums, Discussion Boards, and Q&A Sections

The website includes various forums and discussion boards where you can ask questions, provide answers, and engage with others in the AI and LLM agent development community. Whether you are troubleshooting a problem or sharing your latest project, these forums provide a collaborative space to learn from others.

- **Community Forum**: A place to discuss concepts from the book, share insights, and collaborate with other readers. You can ask questions about specific code examples or theoretical topics, and members of the community, including the authors, can offer guidance.

    Example of how to ask a question on the forum:

    - **Topic**: "Trouble integrating the memory module with LLMs."
    - **Question**: "I've followed the steps in Chapter 6, but I'm encountering issues when trying to maintain context between messages. Can anyone provide advice or suggestions?"
- **Q&A Section**: This section is designed for quick queries where users can post specific technical questions or challenges they are facing. The answers are community-driven, with contributions from both beginners and experts in the field.

    Example:

    - **Question**: "What's the best way to handle tokenization with large datasets?"
    - **Answer**: "You can use the `transformers` library's batch encoding functions, which will help you handle large datasets more efficiently."
- **Webinars and Live Sessions**: Periodically, the companion website will host webinars or live Q&A sessions with the authors and guest experts. These sessions allow you to ask questions in real-time and get clarification on complex topics.

Accessing the Community Forum:

- **Join the Forum**: Visit the Forum
- **Q&A Section**: Ask a Question

---

3. Updates and Errata

As technology evolves, so too do the best practices, tools, and libraries used to develop LLM agents. To ensure that the information you have is up-to-date and accurate, the companion website will provide regular updates to the book's content. Additionally, any errata (errors or corrections) will be posted promptly, ensuring you always have access to the most current and correct information.

Latest Updates to the Book's Content

The companion website will feature a dedicated section where you can find the latest updates to the content of the book. These updates could include:

- **New versions of code**: As libraries and frameworks are updated (e.g., TensorFlow, PyTorch, Hugging Face), code snippets and examples from the book will be updated to reflect these changes.
- **New developments in LLM technology**: As new models, such as GPT-4 or newer, are released, the book will include additional chapters or sections discussing these advancements.

Corrections and Clarifications

As part of the commitment to providing accurate and error-free content, any corrections to previously published material will be posted in this section. If there are minor mistakes in code examples, clarifications for complex concepts, or changes based on new developments, these will be addressed.

- **Errata**: If you find a mistake or clarification is needed in a section, you can view the updated corrections here. Example:
  - **Correction to Chapter 5**: "In the original example for model training, we had omitted the `num_train_epochs` parameter. This is now corrected, and the proper code should include `num_train_epochs=3`."

How to Check for Updates and Errata:

- **View the Latest Updates**: Visit Updates Section
- **Errata**: View Errata

The companion website provides critical resources and ongoing support for readers of this book. With access to code repositories, templates, downloadable PDFs, forums, and live sessions, you can continue to build on the foundation provided here and enhance your practical knowledge. Additionally, the updates and errata section ensures that the content remains current, enabling you to stay aligned with the latest developments in the field of LLM agents. By engaging with the community and staying up-to-date with the newest information, you can maximize your learning experience and continue growing as an AI practitioner.